Culinary Arts Institute ®

THE
BUDGET
COOKBOOK

Featured in cover photo:
Meat Loaf à la Wellington, page 48

THE
BUDGET

THE BUDGET COOKBOOK

The Culinary Arts Institute Staff:

Helen Geist: Director

Sherrill Corley and Barbara MacDonald: Editors

Ethel La Roche: Editorial Assistant • Ivanka Simatic: Recipe Tester

Edward Finnegan: Executive Editor • Malinda Miller: Copy Editor

Charles Bozett: Art Director

Book designed and coordinated by Charles Bozett and Laurel DiGangi

Illustrations by Deborah Glaubke

Adventures in Cooking SERIES

COOKBOOK

Culinary Arts Institute®

1975 North Hawthorne, Melrose Park, Illinois 60160

Library of Congress Catalog Card Number: 76-3308
International Standard Book Number: 0-8326-0550-6
International Standard Book Number (Hard Cover): 0-8326-0557-3

ACKNOWLEDGMENTS

American Dairy Association; California Apricot Advisory Board;
Florida Department of Citrus; Frozen Potato Products Institute;
National Fisheries Institute; National Macaroni Institute;
The Quaker Oats Company

TEST YOUR FOOD BUYING IQ

T F 1. Meat graded Prime or Choice is more tender than meat graded Good.

T F 2. Large eggs are a better buy than medium eggs when they are priced no more than 10 percent higher than medium eggs.

T F 3. The best way to determine which of two cuts of meat will give the most for your money is to divide weight into price. The one giving the most weight per dollar is the best buy.

T F 4. You won't save much money, if any, by home canning unless you do it for several years, even if you grow your own food.

T F 5. Enriched flour is more nutritious than whole-grain flour.

T F 6. The average American adult should eat more red meat for protein.

T F 7. When a 2-pound box of instant mashed potatoes is priced below a 10-pound bag of potatoes, the instant potatoes are a better buy.

T F 8. It costs more to serve frozen orange juice than to make your own juice from fresh oranges.

T F 9. There is as much iron in a hot-dog bun as in the frank itself.

T F 10. Nonfat dry milk solids can be used either in dry form or reconstituted with water and used as a liquid in recipes.

Turn the page for the answers.

ANSWERS TO FOOD-BUYING IQ TEST

1. **False.** Cuts from all three grades will be tender if properly cooked. Some cuts from Prime and Choice, as well as from Good, classify as "less tender" but become tender through proper cooking. (See page 46.)

2. **True.** Large eggs average 24 ounces per dozen; medium eggs, 21 ounces per dozen. That means that large eggs give 12½ more volume than medium eggs. A 10% difference in price makes the large-sized eggs a good value. (See page 67.)

3. **False.** Figure servings per dollar, not weight per dollar. A bony cut such as spareribs gives fewer servings than a boneless cut, so unless the price is considerably lower, the boneless meat is a better value. (See page 46.)

4. **True.** The cost of the canner, jars, lids, sugar, and cooking fuel must all be figured into the cost of canning. Averaged over the years, home canning can mean savings, especially if you raise your own produce. (See page 14.)

5. **False.** In milling white flour, the nutritious germ and bran are removed; only the endosperm remains. Enrichment returns some of the original nutrients, but not all. (See page 11.)

6. **False.** Most American adults get more protein in the daily diet than they need. However, meat is a rich source of vitamins and minerals, too. If those are obtained from less expensive plant sources, you can cut back on the meat, and lower the food bill at the same time. (See page 12.)

7. **True,** assuming you want to serve mashed potatoes. (See page 14.)

8. **False.** A 12-ounce can of frozen orange juice makes 1½ quarts of juice; the equivalent of juice from 18 oranges. When making frozen orange juice, remember that vitamin C value diminishes on exposure to air. Plan to serve immediately; cover and refrigerate leftovers. (See page 14.)

9. **True.** According to the U.S. Department of Agriculture Bulletin No. 72, each provides an average of .8 milligram of iron. (See page 11.)

10. **True.** It is used to good advantage as a dry ingredient in our Multi-Purpose Baking Mix (page 15); water, not whole milk, is used in its many variations.

CONTENTS

Plan to Save—To Save, Plan 9
    The Best-Laid Plans 10
    Which Brand? 10
    Nutrition Labeling and Other Label Information 10
    Time and Energy 12
    Can She Bake a Cherry Pie? 12

Make or Buy? 13
    Cheaper to Do-It-Yourself 13
    Cheaper to Buy in the Convenience Form 14

Homemade Mixes 15

Substitutions 25

Gourmet Dining on a Budget 27

Budgeting for One or Two 31
    Planning for the Couple 31
    Batching It 31
    Week's Menus 32
    Shopping List 33

Leftovers 35
    The ABC of Leftovers 35
    Recipes 36

Budget-Saving Recipes 41

Soups and Stews 41
Meat 46
  Meat Grading and Inspection 46
  Learn to Figure Servings Per Pound 46
  The Bone Shape Is a Guide to Tenderness 47
  Recipes 47
Fish 54
Poultry 58
Pasta and Other Cereal Dishes 63
Egg and Cheese Dishes 67
  Eggs 67
  Cheese 67
  Recipes 68
Fruits and Vegetables 72
  Fresh Produce 72
  Canned Fruits and Vegetables 72
  Frozen Fruits and Vegetables 72
  Recipes 73
Treats 76
  Snacks 76
  Beverages 78
  Desserts 79

Menu Plans for Two Weeks 83
  Menus for a Family of Four—Week 1 83
  Shopping List 85
  Menus for a Family of Four—Week 2 86
  Shopping List 87

How Long Will It Keep? 89
  Refrigerator Storage 89
  Freezer Storage 90

Index 92

PLAN TO SAVE— TO SAVE, PLAN

Whether or not you knew all the answers to our quiz, you are sure to have firsthand experience with food budgeting. Nearly everyone knows what to do; what's needed is the resolve to do it.

A well-known cartoon shows a character with feet up on the table saying, "Next week we've got to get organized . . ." That's where many of us stand—or sit—on food budgeting.

Take list-making. Everybody knows that a shopping list helps—a list based on meal plans. And that the meal plans should be made with an eye to good nutrition.

Yet, more often than not, the shopper runs out of time and dashes off to the store with only a vague idea of what is needed to put meals on the table. Here's what is lost while "saving" the time of making plans:

Nutrition. Getting all the basics into daily meals rarely happens by accident. First, the planner needs to know which foods furnish the basic nutrients. (For a quick brushup, see page 11.) A session with pencil and paper, deciding on dishes for each meal, is the best way to cover all bases.

Time. The "listless" shopper is apt to forget essential items, and make needless return trips to the store.

Protection against impulse buying. One of the hazards in budgeting is the sudden urge to try something nonessential. With a list in hand (and only so much money in the pocket) the task is easier.

Shop right after eating so hunger doesn't enter the picture. And if possible, shop by yourself. The impulses are multiplied by each child—and adult—in the shopping party.

Thrifty use of leftovers. Our shopper should make food go the full distance by planning leftovers from the start. By taking the time, you can make the most of a plan such as this:

Sunday—Meat ample for serving two meals
Monday—Non-meat main dish
Tuesday—Leftover dish from Sunday's meat
Wednesday—Meat dish to serve just one meal
Thursday—Meat ample for serving two meals
Friday—Non-meat main dish
Saturday—Leftover dish from Thursday's meat

This plan means only three purchases at the meat counter. If you're used to making seven, you can see what a saving that will make. Hike the saving even farther by selecting the week's special.

Not all leftovers are planned; we all have a few surprises, as no one can predict exactly how much the family will eat at any given meal. That's why flexibility is so important in meal plans. More meat left over than you'd bargained for? Use it up in yet another leftover guise to serve on one of those "non-meat main dish" nights.

What if the family eats more than you'd thought, and there isn't enough meat left for the repeat performance? It helps to have a few shelf staple items on hand. Such things as canned tuna, canned soups, and pasta can be used to improvise emergency meals.

Considering all the advantages, it's easy to see that planning is important. But even with all the evidence, some people are simply not plan-makers. If that's your problem, you can still benefit from plans—plans made by somebody else. Check our ready-made weekly menus (page 83 for families, page 32 for singles and couples). Adapt them to your tastes, and give them a try. We've even made up the shopping lists.

After a few weeks of shopping with a plan—either yours or ours—it should become a habit. In time, you may not need complete menus in advance. You may be able to plan just the meats and main dishes, leaving yourself free to buy a predetermined number of items from the produce section, canned and frozen foods departments, bakery, dairy case, and so on. These numbers will be based on the number of servings called for in the complete meal plans, and should agree with the number of items on our shopping lists (pages 33, 85, and 87).

But, you say, you really want to create your own meal plans rather than use ready-made ones. Here is how to go about it.

THE BEST-LAID PLANS

Check cookbooks and newspaper and magazine food pages for ideas. When it comes to final decisions, keep these things in mind:
—Food your family likes
—Food on hand
—Food that gives needed nutrients
—Food that fits your time schedule and skills

Let your family have a voice in meal plans. Even ultracheap food is no bargain if they leave it on the plate. And keep an open mind. Some items that classify as "fun food" are good for you, too. Take pizza—it contains meat, cheese, pastry, and vegetables—foods from all the basic groups! If your family happens to like it, serve it with a clear conscience.

But don't overdo it. No matter how fond they are of a given dish, don't serve it too often. Variety is not only the spice of life, but an essential ingredient in meal planning. Some cooks make it a policy not to serve any dish more than once a month. They may still serve chicken and hamburger once a week, but they vary the recipe.

THE ONCE-A-WEEK INVENTORY AND STOCK TAKING

Another starting point for meal planning is to make an inventory of what you already have on hand.

Time your shopping trip to follow a refrigerator and pantry cleanout. The cleanout prevents food from being shoved to the back and forgotten, and may result in a bonus meal of leftovers. In some homes, cleanout day means soup or stew for dinner. In hot weather, slice the leftover roast for a whole-meal salad.

Your weekly cleanout will also make room for the new supply of groceries.

HOW DOES YOUR PLAN STACK UP?

You've polled the family for preferences, you've checked what you have on hand, and you have a plan on paper. Check it against the chart on page 11. Count the number of servings in each category to make sure you've included an ample amount.

THE MOMENT OF DECISION—WHICH BRAND??

Even after your plan is made, there are decisions to make at the store. If you planned your menus with the newspaper food page in hand, you may have clipped a few coupons for products that will take priority. Or perhaps you've found that chain-store house brands give even better value than advertised brands less the cents-off offer. Before you assume that either is the better buy, take a closer look at this week's price.

And make it a habit to figure cost per serving. Divide the number of servings into the price. The number of servings is often stated on the can or carton of packaged food; see page 46 for meat.

Another consideration is how much your family will eat at a meal. The jumbo size may offer a better price per serving, but if servings are left over to be thrown out, it may pay to buy only what you are sure your family will eat.

Consider value received as well as price. If your family is fond of Brand X, and anything else brings groans of disappointment, the few pennies extra for Brand X may be well spent.

NUTRITION LABELING AND OTHER LABEL INFORMATION

Nutrition labeling has made it easier to know which foods are the most nutritious. The nutrition label (panel) is used on packaged foods and beverages when a nutrient claim is made or nutrients have been added. Other foods may provide nutrition labeling if the manufacturer chooses.

Nutrition labeling won't solve all meal planning problems, since it's not found on every food. Produce from the fresh-air stand, for example, is not labeled, but makes a big contribution to good eating.

Keep in mind that the U.S. Recommended Daily Allowances, the basis for nutrition labeling, are generally based on the highest needs in any category. A full 100 percent of the U.S. RDA is more than

DAILY FOOD GUIDE

FRUIT AND VEGETABLES
4 servings each day to include 1 citrus fruit and
1 dark green or deep yellow fruit or vegetable

**MEAT, FISH, POULTRY,
AND OTHER PROTEIN FOODS GROUP**
2 servings daily

MILK AND DAIRY PRODUCTS GROUP
About 3 servings daily

BREAD AND CEREAL GROUP
4 servings daily

most of us need. It probably wouldn't hurt to get a nutritional overabundance, but it wouldn't benefit us much, either. And the calories that would ride along with those excess nutrients would be far more than most of us can take without weight gain.

So the percentages you find on a nutrition label are not meant to suggest that you collect cartons adding up to 100 percent. They are there to help you make decisions within each category. If you are trying to decide between two products to furnish the day's vitamin C (for example, orange or tomato juice), a look at the label will help—costs and family preferences being equal.

It would be pointless to compare foods in different categories, such as peanut butter and tomato juice. Each is valuable in its own way—peanut butter for protein and tomato juice for vitamin C—and neither should be rejected because it's low in some other nutrient.

Another label guide is the term "enriched" or "whole grain" on bread and cereals. In milling white flour, the nutrient-rich germ and bran are removed, leaving the starchy endosperm only. This removes much of the food value of the grain.

Back in the 1930s, nutritionists became alarmed by evidence of malnutrition in our country. They urged the government to require that flour be enriched. Legislation was passed, and now flour that is used in interstate commerce (virtually all flour) has had thiamine, riboflavin, niacin, and iron restored. Thanks to enrichment, a hot-dog bun provides .8 milligram of iron—as much as in the frank itself!

However, other nutrients that are lost with the

NUTRITION INFORMATION
Serving Size . . . 1 cup (8½ oz.)
Servings per Container . . . 2

Per One-Cup Serving:
Calories 230   Carbohydrate . . 50 grams
Protein . . 4 grams   Fat . . . . 2 grams

**PERCENTAGE OF U.S. RECOMMENDED
DAILY ALLOWANCE (U.S. RDA)**
Protein . . . 6   Thiamine . . . 2   Calcium . . *
Vitamin A . . 4   Riboflavin . . 6   Iron 4
Vitamin C . 20   Niacin 8
*Contains less than 2 percent of the U.S. RDA
of this nutrient.

Nutritional Label for Cream Style Corn

bran and germ are not restored, leading some people to prefer whole-grain products. But white flour has its place; it is essential to the production of white bread, cake, and many other recipes.

With the Basic Food Groups well in mind, buying decisions will come more easily. You may even find that you have been overbuying in certain categories, spending more than was really necessary.

Take meat. Purchases at the meat case account for about a third of each food dollar, yet many Americans get more protein than they really need. Sound surprising? Probably, because we've been told since childhood to eat plenty of red meat. It's advice we enjoy taking.

But we've been oversold. A grown man needs 56 grams of protein daily; a woman, 46. Yet most adults in this country average 80 to 90 grams per day! Clearly, we could cut down on meat, and cut the food bill at the same time.

Food costs could be dropped further by substituting protein foods that are less expensive than meat. Serve fish and chicken dishes regularly, and nonanimal protein foods, too. Such foods as nuts, legumes, beans, rice, and pasta teamed with protein from an animal source such as milk or eggs, help to meet protein needs. Dark green and deep yellow vegetables and fruits can furnish many of the vitamins and minerals found in meat.

With all this in mind, the budget shopper won't overload the cart with high-priced meats. She'll seek out alternatives, and buy only as much protein food as her family really needs.

The Universal Product Code may also be found on labels. This is a symbol of 30 black and 29 white bars with 10 numbers underneath. An optical scan-ner in many stores can read this UPC symbol at the checkout. A computer decodes, totals prices, and makes a detailed print-out receipt.

Open Dating, sometimes called the "pull-date" or the "sell-date," is on some labels. It is set to allow several days of added storage time at home. It is not meant as a "throw-out" date.

THE COOK'S OTHER RESOURCES —TIME AND ENERGY

We're forever hearing that the way to cut food costs is to cook from scratch. That may save money, but it cuts into two other resources: time and energy (yours, and cooking fuel). Working women and others who operate on a tight schedule may feel that budgeting is a lost cause.

If your time in the kitchen is limited, lengthy cooking may not be for you. You'll need to watch for budget foods that are precooked or ones that can be cooked in a hurry. In the meat line, that means such items as fully cooked ham and table-ready meats; or quick-cookers such as hamburger.

Even the working woman can sometimes juggle her time to fit in long cooking sessions. On weekends and weekday evenings she can "cook now—enjoy later," letting the freezer hold the fruits of her labor.

Mechanical aids to the hurried housewife are the microwave oven and the electric slow-cooking pot—in two very different ways. The microwave speeds up cooking so the working wife can put dinner on the table in record time. The pot slows it down, so she can start dinner in the morning before leaving for work.

Both appliances require an investment of money, which could defeat the budgeter's purpose. But they deserve consideration as they could pay for themselves in the long run.

CAN SHE BAKE A CHERRY PIE?

Today's homemaker may not have grown up in a home where basic cooking was practiced; after all, convenience foods have been around for over a generation. Now, suddenly, she is challenged to practice a skill not learned at mother's knee.

For the willing cook, there are ways to make up this deficit. Check the extension and adult education classes in your neighborhood, or have a talent swap with some experienced cook you know. She'd probably love to have you teach her how to knit! Try to gain the know-how as economically as possible. If saving money is your goal, it doesn't make sense to take an expensive course in *haute cuisine.*

MAKE OR BUY?

The supermarket has become a bewildering showcase of convenience foods. There is a packaged mix for nearly everything, in several brands with many variations. And besides the shelves of cans and boxes, there are cases of frozen foods just waiting to be popped into the oven.

Our conscience says that it would be better all around to buy fresh foods and cook them from scratch. We'd conserve money, flavor, and nutrients, right?

The answer isn't that simple. Out-of-season asparagus, obviously, won't be the buy that you'll find in the freezer case. Canned, frozen, and otherwise packaged foods can be marketed economically because they are processed at the peak of the harvest season when price is lowest. Frozen produce may actually retain more food value than the fresh counterparts because they are usually quick-frozen before there is time for nutrient loss.

Economy aside, there can still be good reasons for buying fresh foods and doing your own cooking. People who like food additive-free find it worthwhile even though there may be no cost advantage. Others like the personality of home-cooked food. And the fiber provided by unprocessed food is important, too. Back in Granny's day, "roughage" was highly endorsed; today's nutritionists are reminding us that it is still a diet necessity.

Make or buy? You'll have to make the decision for yourself. But strictly for a cost comparison, consult the following charts. The first shows foods that are cheaper prepared at home. The other lists convenience foods that cost less and provide built-in maid service. These are simple price comparisons; quality is another consideration.

CHEAPER TO DO-IT-YOURSELF

BREADS AND CEREALS

Breakfast cereal	Cheaper to cook hot cereal (regular, not instant) than serve dry cereal. Make your own granola (page 79). Cornmeal is economical, too, and can be served as a hot cereal ("mush") or cooked, refrigerated, sliced, and fried.
Biscuits, muffins, and variations	Use our Multi-Purpose Baking Mix (page 15) and save time as well as money.

MEAT, POULTRY, AND FISH

Whole chicken	Learn to cut up for frying (page 60). Broiler-fryers can often be used in recipes calling for stewing or roasting hens. Save giblets in freezer for making stock. Chop liver for pâté (page 29).
Lunchmeat	Buy whole pieces and slice it yourself.
Sandwich fillings	Use leftover roast, chicken, and fish.

Hamburger sauce	Buy hamburger on special, make sauce on page 19.

PRODUCE

Fruits and vegetables	A bargain at peak of season, but figure in trimming loss.
Nuts	Cheaper to buy unshelled.

SNACK FOODS

Popcorn	A half cup of popcorn costing a few pennies produces a big bowl of snack food.
Fruit drinks	Canned fruit drinks and dry drink mixes, while not cheap, are less than bottled pop. Iced tea, alone or mixed with fruit drinks, is inexpensive.

OTHERS

Chicken seasoned coating mix	Use the variation of Multi-Purpose Baking Mix (page 15).
Cocoa mix	See page 24 for a recipe.
Salad dressings	Recipes start on page 21.
Syrup, artificial maple	Buy maple flavoring in the flavoring extract section at the grocery store, and follow label directions.

CHEAPER TO BUY IN THE CONVENIENCE FORM

BREAD

Commercially baked loaves	These represent a time- and fuel-rather than a price-saving. The little saved on price by home-baking is partially lost in oven fuel. Excellent savings can be made by buying day-old bread.

PRODUCE

Bottled lemon juice	Cheaper cost and longer storage life than fresh lemons.

Commercially canned and frozen fruits and vegetables	Except for the height of the harvest, commercially processed fruits and vegetables are nearly always cheaper and have no trimming loss. Home canners must add the price of jars, lids, sugar, and cooking fuel to the price of the food. If you can for many years, and grow your own produce, you will save. Home freezing must also spread the price of the freezer over many years to realize a saving. Vegetables in large, resealable poly-bags are economical.
Frozen orange juice	A 12-ounce can makes 1½ quarts; equivalent to, but cheaper than, about 1½ dozen oranges.
Freeze-dried, dried, and frozen vegetables and herbs	In addition to low cost, these items have a longer storage life than the fresh products.
Instant mashed potatoes	Compare the prices of a 2-pound package and a 10-pound bag of potatoes. Since the yield is similar, let the price decide.

FISH

Canned fish	Mackerel, tuna, and sometimes salmon produce budget main dishes.

SNACKS AND DESSERTS

Packaged pudding mix and flavored gelatin	These produce economical after-school snacks and mealtime desserts.
Ice cream	Standard quality (not fancy) is cheaper than homemade. Ice milk is an even better bargain.
Cake mixes	While not as cheap as our Family Cake (page 16) they cost less than from-scratch cakes using cake flour.

HOMEMADE MIXES

When you buy a packaged mix, you know you're making a trade-off: money for time. The mix represents a savings in time—and time, for certain people, is as scarce as money.

But when it's money that's in short supply, it's possible to have your mix and your money, too. The answer is to make your own mix.

Mixes can be made in many varieties. There is a homemade one for biscuits so versatile it doubles as a mix for a myriad of other things, and one mix for nearly everything else that requires a recipe.

But you have only so much shelf space, and only a limited need for certain recipes. These factors help to determine how many mixes it is practical to make.

The Multi-Purpose Baking Mix (page 15) deserves shelf space because it has so many uses. A basic Hamburger Mix (page 19), also with multiple uses, is worth making in quantity and freezing. Salad Dressing Mixes (pages 21 and 24) can be put into regular use, too.

The desirability of additional mixes depends on the preference of the cook. If you happen to like serving up hot breads regularly, specialty items such as the Basic Oats Mix (page 20) will earn its shelf space.

The amount you save, using homemade mixes, depends on how often you use them. Use them frequently, and they will make a dramatic difference over the long term.

Carry the homemade mix story to its logical conclusion by making your own storage canisters. Save large cans that come with reusable plastic lids, such as shortening and coffee cans. Wash and dry them thoroughly, cover them with adhesive-backed decorative paper, if desired, and label.

Multi-Purpose Baking Mix

2 pounds (about 8 cups) all-purpose flour
1¼ cups instant nonfat dry milk solids
¼ cup (4 tablespoons) baking powder
1 tablespoon salt
2 cups shortening

1. Combine flour, dry milk solids, baking powder, and salt in a large mixing bowl.
2. Cut shortening into dry ingredients with pastry blender or two knives until mixture resembles coarse cornmeal.
3. Store in tightly covered container in a cool place.
4. Before measuring for use in recipe, lighten mix by tossing with fork. Do not pack when measuring.

About 12 cups mix

Baking Powder Biscuits

    3 cups Multi-Purpose Baking Mix (page 15)
    ¾ cup water

1. Turn Baking Mix into a bowl; make well in mix. Add water and stir until dough follows fork. Gently form dough into a ball.
2. Turn onto lightly floured surface. To knead, fold opposite side of dough over toward you; press lightly with fingertips and turn dough quarter turn. Repeat 10 to 15 times.
3. Gently roll out dough from center to edge until about ½ inch thick. Cut dough with floured cutter or knife, using an even pressure to keep sides of biscuits straight. Place biscuits on ungreased baking sheet.
4. Bake at 450°F about 10 minutes, or until golden brown.

20 (2-inch) biscuits

Chicken Baked with Seasoned Coating Mix

    1 cup Multi-Purpose Baking Mix (page 15)
  1½ teaspoons salt
    1 teaspoon paprika
    ½ teaspoon poultry seasoning
    1 broiler-fryer chicken (2½ to 3 pounds), cut up and rinsed
    ½ cup undiluted evaporated milk or 2 egg whites mixed with 2 teaspoons water

1. Combine Baking Mix, salt, paprika, and poultry seasoning in a shallow bowl.
2. Dip chicken in evaporated milk or egg white in a shallow bowl, then in seasoned mix.
3. Arrange chicken pieces in a shallow 3-quart baking dish.
4. Bake at 375°F 1 hour, or until chicken is tender.

4 to 6 servings

Pancakes

  1½ cups Multi-Purpose Baking Mix (page 15)
    ¾ cup water
    1 egg, slightly beaten

1. Blend Baking Mix, water, and egg.
2. Drop from tablespoon onto hot lightly greased griddle. Cook until bubbles appear; turn and cook other side. Serve at once.

9 to 12 pancakes

Family Cake with Broiled Topping

Cake:
    2 cups Multi-Purpose Baking Mix (page 15)
    ¾ cup sugar
    ½ cup water
    ½ teaspoon vanilla extract
    1 egg
Broiled Topping:
    ⅓ cup packed brown sugar
    1 to 2 tablespoons cocoa
    1 tablespoon milk
    ½ cup chopped nuts
    1 tablespoon soft shortening

1. Blend Baking Mix and sugar in mixing bowl.
2. Add water and vanilla. Beat until well mixed by hand, or about 2 minutes on medium speed of electric mixer.
3. Add egg and continue to beat until well mixed by hand, or about 1 minute on medium speed.
4. Pour batter into a greased and floured 8-inch square pan.

Basic Oats Mix; Fluffy Dumplings;
Quick Applesauce Bread;
Oatmeal Muffins; Oatmeal Biscuits

5. Bake at 375°F 25 to 30 minutes, or until cake springs back when lightly touched at center. Do not remove cake from pan.

6. For broiled topping, mash brown sugar and cocoa together in mixing bowl until there are no cocoa lumps. Add milk and stir until well combined. Stir in nuts and shortening.

7. When cake has cooled slightly, spread with topping mixture. Place under broiler with surface of cake about 4 inches from heat. Broil until topping bubbles. Watch carefully to avoid scorching.

One 8-inch square cake

Lemon Cake

    4 cups Multi-Purpose Baking Mix (page 15)
 1½ cups sugar
   1 cup water
  ¼ cup lemon juice
   2 eggs

1. Combine Baking Mix and sugar in mixing bowl.

2. Add water and lemon juice; stir until well combined, then beat 2 minutes on medium speed of electric mixer.

3. Add eggs and beat 2 minutes longer on medium speed.

4. Pour batter into 2 greased and floured 8- or 9-inch round cake pans, or a 13×9×2-inch cake pan.

5. Bake at 375°F 20 to 25 minutes, or until cake springs back when lightly touched.

6. Frost cooled cake as desired.

One 13×9-inch cake or one 2-layer cake

Waffles

   2 eggs
   1 cup water
   1 tablespoon melted shortening
   2 cups Multi-Purpose Baking Mix (page 15)

1. Beat eggs until frothy. Add water and shortening and stir to combine.

2. Add Baking Mix to liquid and stir until lumps are small but batter is not smooth. Bake in heated waffle baker following manufacturer's directions.

About 4 waffles

Chocolate Cake

    4 cups Multi-Purpose Baking Mix (page 15)
 1½ cups sugar
   6 tablespoons cocoa
 1⅓ cups water
   2 tablespoons vegetable oil
   2 teaspoons vanilla extract
   2 eggs

1. Stir Baking Mix, sugar, and cocoa together in mixing bowl until evenly combined.

2. Add water, oil, and vanilla; stir until well combined, then beat 2 minutes on medium speed of electric mixer.

3. Add eggs and beat 2 minutes longer on medium speed. Pour batter into 2 greased and floured 8- or 9-inch round cake pans, or a 13×9×2-inch cake pan.

4. Bake at 375°F 20 to 25 minutes, or until cake springs back when lightly touched.

5. Frost cooled cake as desired.

One 13×9-inch cake or one 2-layer cake

Nutty Chocolate Pudding

Batter:
1½ cups Multi-Purpose Baking Mix (page 15)
½ cup sugar
2 tablespoons cocoa
¾ cup chopped nuts
½ cup water
1 teaspoon vanilla extract

Topping:
¼ cup cocoa
¾ cup packed brown sugar
1½ cups boiling water

1. For batter, combine Baking Mix, sugar, cocoa, and nuts. Stir in water and vanilla. Spread batter in a greased 8-inch square baking pan.
2. For topping, stir cocoa and brown sugar together until smooth. Add boiling water gradually, stirring until sugar is dissolved. Pour over batter. (Go ahead, even though it looks very runny.)
3. Bake at 350°F about 40 minutes. Serve warm with topping, if desired.

About 9 servings

Fruit Crisp

4 cups prepared fruit, such as sliced apples, peaches, or pears
2 tablespoons water
¼ to ⅓ cup sugar, depending on tartness of fruit

Topping:
1 cup Multi-Purpose Baking Mix (page 15)
¼ cup sugar
½ teaspoon cinnamon
Pinch nutmeg
1 egg

1. Place fruit in a greased 8-inch square baking pan. Mix water and sugar, and spoon over fruit.
2. Combine Baking Mix, sugar, cinnamon, and nutmeg.
3. Beat egg and add gradually to mix, stirring with a fork until mixture is crumbly. Sprinkle over fruit.
4. Bake at 400°F about 25 minutes, or until golden brown.

6 servings

Fruit Cobbler

1 cup Multi-Purpose Baking Mix (page 15)
1 tablespoon sugar
¼ cup water
1 can (about 20 ounces) fruit pie filling, such as cherry, apple, or peach

1. In ovenproof saucepan, heat pie filling until hot and bubbly.
2. Meanwhile, prepare soft dough of Baking Mix, sugar, and water.
3. Drop dough by spoonfuls onto the heated fruit filling.
4. Bake at 425°F 15 to 20 minutes, or until topping is golden brown. Serve warm with whipped topping, ice cream, or milk, if desired.

4 or 5 servings

Pie Crust Mix

6 cups all-purpose flour
1 tablespoon salt
2 cups shortening or lard

1. Mix flour and salt. Cut in 1 cup shortening until the texture is like cornmeal. Cut in remaining cup of shortening till the pieces are the size of small peas.
2. Store mix in tightly covered container, such as two-pound coffee can or two-quart canister.

Enough mix for about six 9-inch pie shells

Pastry for 1-Crust Pie

2 to 3 tablespoons cold water
1½ cups Pie Crust Mix (page 18)

1. Sprinkle 2 to 3 tablespoons cold water over 1½ cups Pie Crust Mix, a teaspoonful at a time, mixing lightly with a fork after each addition. Add only enough water to hold pastry together. Do not overhandle.
2. Shape into a ball and flatten on a lightly floured surface.
3. Roll from center to edge into a round about ⅛ inch thick and 1 inch larger than overall size of pan.
4. Loosen pastry from surface with spatula and fold in quarters. Gently lay pastry in pan and unfold, fitting it into pan so it is not stretched.
5. Trim edge so pastry extends about ½ inch beyond edge of pan. Fold under at edge and flute.
6. If baked shell is desired, prick in several places with fork.
7. Bake at 450°F 10 to 15 minutes, or until crust is light golden brown. Check pastry frequently during baking. If blisters appear, prick with fork to flatten and return crust to oven.

One 8- or 9-inch pie shell

Pastry for 2-Crust Pie

4 to 5 tablespoons cold water
3 cups Pie Crust Mix (page 18)

1. Sprinkle cold water over Pie Crust Mix and proceed as above; dividing pastry into halves. Roll first half and fit into pan as for single crust pie; omit fluting edge and pricking with fork.
2. For top crust, roll out pastry 1 inch larger than pan. Slit pastry in several places to allow steam to escape during baking.
3. Fill bottom crust as recipe directs; cut at edge of pan and moisten for tight seal. Carefully arrange top crust over filling; press edges to seal. Fold extra top pastry under bottom pastry. Flute edges and bake as recipe directs.

One 8- or 9-inch pie

Hamburger Mix

4 pounds hamburger or ground beef
4 medium onions, chopped (about 4 cups)
1 cup chopped celery with tops
2 bottles (12 or 14 ounces each) ketchup
  (about 3 cups)

1 tablespoon salt
½ teaspoon pepper

1. In a Dutch oven, brown hamburger; when some drippings have collected, add chopped onion and celery. Cook until the meat is no longer pink and the vegetables are tender. Drain off excess fat.
2. Add ketchup, salt, and pepper. Simmer 20 minutes.

5 pints mix

To freeze: Cool mixture in refrigerator. Spoon into freezer storage containers with tight lids. Store in freezer.

To thaw: Place container of mix in hot water just long enough to loosen around edges so it will slip out of container. Heat in saucepan or according to recipe.

Sloppy Joes: Heat 1 pint (2 cups) **Hamburger Mix** in a saucepan. To serve, spoon on toast or bread.

Spaghetti Sauce: Put desired amount of **Hamburger Mix** into a saucepan and mix in a dash each of **cayenne pepper** and **garlic salt**; heat thoroughly. Serve on hot **cooked spaghetti** and top with grated cheese, if desired.

Stuffed Cabbage Leaves: Cook 12 to 14 cabbage leaves 5 minutes in a saucepan with boiling salted water; drain. Divide 1 pint (2 cups) **Hamburger Mix** evenly on the leaves, putting a spoonful into the center of each leaf. Fold edges in and roll up. Put roll-ups, folded side down, into a skillet or large saucepan and pour 1 cup (8-ounce can) **tomato sauce** over them. Cover; simmer 15 minutes, or until thoroughly heated.

4 to 6 servings

Quick Chili con Carne: Heat 1 pint (2 cups) Hamburger Mix with 1 can (about 15 ounces) red kidney beans, undrained, and 1 tablespoon chili powder or to taste.

About 4 servings

Meaty Roll-Ups

2 cups Multi-Purpose Baking Mix (page 15)
1 egg
2 cups water
1 pint (2 cups) Hamburger Mix (page 19)
½ to 1 cup finely shredded Cheddar cheese (about 2 to 4 ounces)

1. Make pancake batter using Baking Mix, egg, and water. Bake 6-inch pancakes on hot, lightly greased griddle or skillet.
2. Heat Hamburger Mix. Put a spoonful of Hamburger Mix on each pancake.
3. Roll pancakes and place seam-side down in a greased 3-quart baking dish. Sprinkle with cheese.
4. Bake at 350°F about 10 minutes, or until heated through.

6 servings

Sauced Pinwheels

1 pint (2 cups) Hamburger Mix (page 19)
¼ cup ketchup
2 cups Multi-Purpose Baking Mix (page 15)
⅔ cup water (about)
⅔ cup (about ½ can) condensed tomato soup
¼ cup milk

1. Combine Hamburger Mix and ketchup; set aside.
2. Make soft dough of Baking Mix and water, stirring with fork about 25 strokes. Roll dough into a rectangle ½-inch thick.
3. Spread dough with meat mixture to within ½ inch of edge. Roll up, beginning at wide side of rectangle. Pinch edge of dough to seal well.
4. Cut roll into 6 even slices and arrange on sides in greased 11×7-inch baking pan.
5. Bake at 425°F about 25 minutes.
6. Meanwhile, combine tomato soup and milk; heat.
7. Remove pinwheels from oven. Serve with sauce.

4 to 6 servings

Meat 'n' Biscuit Bake

1 pint (2 cups) Hamburger Mix (page 19)
½ cup shredded Cheddar cheese (about 2 ounces)
1 egg, slightly beaten
2 cups Multi-Purpose Baking Mix (page 15)
¼ cup mayonnaise
⅔ cup water (about)

1. Put Hamburger Mix into mixing bowl. Stir in cheese and egg; mix well.
2. Make soft dough of Baking Mix, mayonnaise, and water, stirring with fork about 25 strokes. Spread half of dough into a well-greased 8-inch square pan.
3. Cover dough with meat mixture.
4. Spoon remaining dough over meat mixture.
5. Bake at 400°F 25 to 30 minutes.
6. Cut into squares and serve hot.

About 6 servings

Basic Oats Mix

6 cups sifted all-purpose flour
¼ cup (4 tablespoons) baking powder
4 teaspoons salt
1⅓ cups shortening
2 cups quick or old-fashioned oats, uncooked

1. Sift flour, baking powder, and salt together into large bowl. Cut in shortening until mixture resembles coarse crumbs. Stir in oats.
3. Store mixture in an air-tight container in a cool, dry place until ready to use.

9¾ cups Mix

Oatmeal Biscuits

    2 cups Basic Oats Mix (page 20)
    ⅔ cup cold milk

1. Combine Oats Mix and milk in a bowl; stir with a fork to a soft dough.
2. Turn dough onto a lightly floured surface. Knead with fingertips 10 times. Roll out to ½-inch thickness. Cut with a floured 2-inch round cutter. Put onto an ungreased cookie sheet.
3. Bake at 450°F 8 to 10 minutes.

About 16 biscuits

Oatmeal Muffins

    2 cups plus 2 tablespoons Basic Oats Mix
        (page 20)
    ¼ cup sugar
    1 cup milk
    1 egg, beaten

1. Combine Oats Mix and sugar in a bowl. Add milk and egg; stir until just blended.
2. Fill 12 greased 2½-inch muffin-pan wells ⅔ full.
3. Bake at 400°F about 20 minutes, or until golden brown.

12 muffins

Quick Applesauce Bread

    2¼ cups Basic Oats Mix (page 20)
     1 cup sugar
     1 teaspoon cinnamon
     1 cup canned sweetened applesauce
     1 egg
     ½ cup milk
     ½ cup raisins

1. Combine Oats Mix, sugar, and cinnamon in a bowl. Add applesauce, egg, milk, and raisins; stir until mixed.
2. Turn batter into a greased and floured 8½×4½×2½-inch loaf pan.
3. Bake at 350°F 55 to 60 minutes.
4. Remove from pan and cool completely on a rack before slicing.

1 loaf bread

Fluffy Dumplings

    2 cups Basic Oats Mix (page 20)
    1 cup milk

Thoroughly combine Oats Mix and milk. Spoon onto boiling stew. Cook, uncovered, over low heat 10 minutes; cover and cook 10 minutes longer.

10 to 12 dumplings

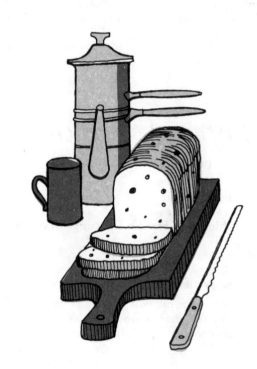

French Dressing Mix

    ¼ cup (4 tablespoons) sugar
    1 tablespoon plus 1 teaspoon salt
    1 tablespoon plus 1 teaspoon paprika
    1 tablespoon plus 1 teaspoon dry mustard
    ½ teaspoon pepper

1. Combine ingredients in jar with tight-fitting lid for storage.
2. At serving time, make 1 cup of French Dressing by combining ¾ cup salad oil, ¼ cup vinegar, and 1 tablespoon of the dry mixed ingredients. Shake in a jar or whirl in the blender.
3. Store unused French Dressing Mix in a tightly covered container.

Enough mix for 8 cups dressing

Curried French Dressing

¾ cup salad oil
¼ cup vinegar
1 tablespoon French Dressing Mix (page 21)
¼ teaspoon curry powder

Combine salad oil, vinegar, French Dressing Mix, and curry powder. Shake together or whirl in a blender.

1 cup dressing

Chiffonade French Dressing

¾ cup salad oil
¼ cup vinegar
1 tablespoon French Dressing Mix (page 21)
1 hard-cooked egg, chopped
2 tablespoons finely chopped ripe olives
4 teaspoons finely chopped parsley

1. Combine salad oil, vinegar, and French Dressing Mix. Shake together or whirl in a blender.
2. Stir in chopped egg, olives, and parsley. Mix well.

1¼ cups dressing

Blue Cheese French Dressing

3 ounces (about ¾ cup) crumbled blue cheese
2 teaspoons water
¾ cup salad oil
¼ cup vinegar
1 tablespoon French Dressing Mix (page 21)

1. Blend the blue cheese and water until smooth.
2. Combine salad oil, vinegar, and French Dressing Mix.
3. Add dressing slowly to cheese, blending after each addition.

About 2 cups dressing

Lorenzo French Dressing

¾ cup salad oil
¼ cup vinegar
1 tablespoon French Dressing Mix (page 21)
¼ cup finely chopped watercress
2 tablespoons chili sauce

Combine salad oil, vinegar, French Dressing Mix, watercress, and chili sauce. Shake together or whirl in a blender.

About 1¼ cups dressing

Garlic French Dressing

¾ cup salad oil
¼ cup vinegar
1 tablespoon French Dressing Mix (page 21)
1 clove garlic, cut in halves

1. Combine salad oil, vinegar, French Dressing

Mix, and garlic halves. Shake together or whirl in a blender.

2. Chill dressing about 12 hours before using to allow flavors to blend. If you did not use blender, remove garlic before serving, or when flavor of dressing is sufficiently strong.

1 cup dressing

French Dressing with Herbs

- ¾ cup salad oil
- ¼ cup vinegar
- 1 tablespoon French Dressing Mix (see page 21)
- 1 teaspoon chopped parsley
- 1 teaspoon chopped chives
- ½ teaspoon chervil
- ½ teaspoon tarragon

Combine all ingredients in a jar with a tight cover and shake well, or whirl in a blender.

About 1 cup dressing

Tomato French Dressing

- ¾ cup salad oil
- ¼ cup vinegar
- 2 tablespoons ketchup
- 1 tablespoon French Dressing Mix (see page 21)
- 1 teaspoon Worcestershire sauce
- ¼ green pepper, finely chopped

Combine all ingredients, except green pepper, in a jar with a tight cover and shake well, or whirl in a blender. Mix in green pepper.

About 1¼ cups dressing

Vinaigrette French Dressing

- ¾ cup salad oil
- ¼ cup vinegar
- 1 tablespoon French Dressing Mix (see page 21)
- 2 tablespoons finely chopped dill pickle

- 2 teaspoons chopped chives
- 1 hard-cooked egg, chopped

1. Combine salad oil, vinegar, and French Dressing Mix in a jar with a tight cover and shake well, or whirl in a blender.

2. Add pickle, chives, and hard-cooked egg; stir to combine.

About 1½ cups dressing

Honey French Dressing for Fruit

- ¾ cup salad oil
- ½ cup honey
- ¼ cup vinegar
- 1 tablespoon French Dressing Mix (page 21)
- ½ teaspoon celery seed
- ¼ teaspoon grated lemon peel

1. Combine ingredients in jar and shake well or whirl in blender.

2. Serve over **fruit salad**. Store unused portion covered in refrigerator.

1½ cups dressing

Onion French Dressing

¾ cup salad oil
¼ cup vinegar
1 tablespoon French Dressing Mix (page 21)
½ cup (1 medium) minced onion

Combine salad oil, vinegar, French Dressing Mix, and onion. Shake together or whirl in a blender.

About 1½ cups dressing

Greek Salad

½ cup salad oil
3 tablespoons lemon juice
1 tablespoon Italian Dressing Mix (see above)
1 teaspoon oregano
2 quarts mixed greens
2 medium tomatoes, cut in wedges
½ cup ripe olives
½ cup feta cheese
1 can (2 ounces) anchovy fillets

1. In jar, shake together oil, lemon juice, Italian Dressing Mix, and oregano.
2. In salad bowl, toss together the greens, tomatoes, and ¼ cup each of the ripe olives and feta cheese, with enough dressing to coat lightly.

3. Garnish with remaining olives, cheese, and anchovy fillets.

6 to 8 servings

Italian Dressing Mix

1 tablespoon plus 1 teaspoon salt
3 teaspoons garlic powder or instant minced garlic
2 teaspoons pepper

1. Combine ingredients in small jar with tight-fitting lid for storage.
2. When ready to use, make 1¼ cups of Italian Dressing by combining ¾ cup salad oil, 6 tablespoons wine vinegar, and 1 tablespoon of the mixed dry ingredients. Shake in a jar or whirl in the blender.
3. Store unused Italian Dressing Mix in a tightly covered container.

Enough mix for 3 cups dressing

Anchovy Dressing

Combine 1 teaspoon prepared mustard and 2 anchovy fillets with Italian Dressing.

Blue Cheese Dressing

Combine 4 ounces (about 1 cup) blue cheese, ½ teaspoon sugar, and ½ teaspoon dry mustard with Italian Dressing.

Cocoa Mix

4 cups instant nonfat dry milk solids
½ cup plus 2 tablespoons sugar
½ cup unsweetened cocoa
⅛ teaspoon salt

1. Mix all ingredients in a bowl until the cocoa is well distributed.
2. Store in a jar with a tight-fitting lid.
3. To make hot cocoa, stir mix and combine ⅓ cup mix with ⅔ cup boiling water in heatproof cup. Stir well until cocoa powder is completely dissolved. Serve topped with marshmallows, if desired.

About 5 cups mix or enough for about 15 cups hot cocoa

SUBSTITUTIONS

"Cooking with butter" has become synonymous with "cooking with love." Some people feel that cooking with anything less than the best—and most expensive—ingredients amounts to short-changing the family.

That's a costly hangup. Often you can achieve equal—if different—results using a lower-cost substitute. "Different," because any change of ingredient will alter the finished dish in some way. But it might even be an improvement. Some people like skim milk better than whole; others prefer ice milk to ice cream—both usually lower-cost substitutes.

Use the following chart with discrimination. Note which substitutes are to be made in cooked recipes only, for example. With care and practice, you will find many alternatives that will make a real difference in your food budget.

Not all substitutes represent a significant saving at all times of year and in all locations. Supply and demand do control prices. And some substitutes will save only a few pennies, but as penny watchers know, save enough and the dollars will take care of themselves.

SUBSTITUTE AND SAVE

(Note: Using a substitute gives a slightly different, but satisfactory, result)

Baking powder (1 teaspoon)	½ teaspoon cream of tartar + ¼ teaspoon baking soda; or ¼ teaspoon soda + ½ cup sour milk
Beef broth (1 cup)	1 beef bouillon cube + 1 cup hot water; or 1 cup canned beef broth or bouillon; or 1 teaspoon instant beef bouillon + 1 cup hot water
Bread crumbs, dry (¼ cup)	¼ cup cracker crumbs or corn-meal; or ⅔ cup rolled oats; or 1 cup soft bread crumbs
Butter (1 cup)	1 cup margarine; or ⅞ to 1 cup vegetable shortening + ½ teaspoon salt; or ⅞ cup lard + ½ teaspoon salt
Cereal (Chocolate farina)	Add ½ teaspoon dry cocoa per serving to dry cereal and mix well; proceed with package cooking instructions
Cheese, natural (such as Cheddar or Swiss)	Equal amount of pasteurized process cheese (1 cup shredded or grated cheese equals about 4 ounces cheese)
Chicken broth (1 cup)	1 chicken bouillon cube + 1 cup hot water; or 1 teaspoon instant chicken bouillon + 1 cup hot water; or 1 cup canned chicken broth; or cooking liquid from simmered chicken
Chicken, cooked (5 cups)	Two cans (3 pounds 4 ounces each) whole chicken; or 7 cans or jars (5 ounces each) cooked chicken; or 1 cooked stewing chicken (4 to 5 pounds); or 2 frying chickens (2 to 3 pounds each) simmered

Chocolate, unsweetened (1 ounce)	3 tablespoons cocoa + 1 tablespoon shortening	**Marshmallows (10 miniature)**	1 large marshmallow
Chocolate pieces, semisweet (½ cup) for melting only	3 ounces (3 squares) semisweet chocolate	**Milk, whole (1 cup)**	1 cup reconstituted nonfat dry milk + 2 teaspoons margarine or butter; or ½ cup undiluted evaporated milk + ½ cup water
Cornstarch (1 tablespoon)	2 tablespoons flour	**Milk, sour (1 cup)**	1 tablespoon lemon juice or vinegar + enough milk to make 1 cup
Cream, half-and-half (1 cup)	⅞ cup milk plus 3 tablespoons margarine or butter	**Mustard, prepared (1 teaspoon)**	½ teaspoon dry mustard
Cream, sour (1 cup)	1 tablespoon vinegar or lemon juice plus enough evaporated milk to make 1 cup. Let stand 5 minutes before using; stir. Use for cooked recipe ingredient only.	**Oil, for frying (¼ cup)**	¼ cup melted margarine or butter; or ¼ cup bacon drippings, melted; or ¼ cup vegetable shortening or lard, melted
Cream, whipping (for whipped use)	Evaporated milk, when chilled to the ice crystal stage, can be whipped, using chilled bowl and beaters, to give almost 3 times its original volume (whipping cream doubles when whipped). A 13-ounce can gives about 4½ cups whipped milk.	**Onion, 1 medium (½ cup chopped)**	2 tablespoons onion salt (reduce salt in recipe); or 2 tablespoons instant minced onion or onion flakes; or 1½ teaspoons onion powder
Cream, whipping	¾ cup whole milk plus ⅓ cup margarine or butter (to be used as liquid ingredient, not whipped)	**Sugar, brown (1 cup)**	1 cup white sugar (only in recipes that don't depend on flavor and color of brown sugar for success)
Flour, cake (1 cup)	⅞ cup (or 1 cup minus 2 tablespoons) all-purpose flour	**Sugar, confectioners' (1¼ cups)**	1 cup granulated sugar blended at high speed until pulverized
Flour for thickening (1 tablespoon)	½ tablespoon cornstarch; or 2 teaspoons quick-cooking tapioca	**Tomato juice (1 cup)**	½ cup tomato sauce + ½ cup water; use for recipe ingredient
Garlic (1 clove)	⅛ teaspoon garlic powder; or ½ teaspoon garlic salt (reduce salt in recipe by ¼ teaspoon)	**Tomato ketchup or chili sauce (1 cup)**	1 cup tomato sauce + ½ cup sugar and 2 tablespoons vinegar; use for cooked recipe ingredient
Herbs, fresh (1 tablespoon)	1 teaspoon dried herbs	**Tomato sauce (1 cup)**	¾ cup tomato paste + ¼ cup water
Honey (1 cup)	1¼ cup sugar + ¼ cup liquid (water, juice, etc.); use in recipes only	**Tomatoes, cooked (2 cups)**	1 can (16 ounces) tomatoes; use for cooked recipe ingredient
		Yeast, compressed (1 cake)	1 package or 2 teaspoons active dry yeast

GOURMET DINING ON A BUDGET

It's hard for some people to get down to serious "budget cooking" because the term carries overtones of privation. Sure, we can cut back—whenever we get used to the idea of doing without.

So it comes as a bit of a surprise to learn that many recipes that classify as "gourmet" started out as budget cooking. Some are generations old, created by thrifty cooks who were operating on a shoestring. Whatever was grown, caught, or raised locally determined the daily fare.

Yet these cooks suffered from no shortage of inspiration. They knew how to bring out the best in whatever they prepared. Meat was scarce, and what little they had was apt to be tough. They extended it in vegetable combinations (glorified stews) and simmered it to tenderness in heavenly sauces.

The wine they so frequently used in cooking was not a luxury; it was probably homemade. When we duplicate their efforts, we are well advised to use a good, but inexpensive, everyday wine.

The lowly egg was elevated to "haute cuisine" through such inventions as the soufflé and quiche. Even the daily bread gained gourmet stature in the creation of brioche.

So whether food is classified as gourmet or merely penny-pinching seems to hinge on the presence of one ingredient—imagination. Here is a collection of celebrity recipes so impressive that no one will notice they are also "budget cooking."

Sauerbraten

1 beef blade pot roast (3 to 4 pounds)
1 clove garlic, halved
2 teaspoons salt
¼ teaspoon pepper
2 cups cider vinegar
2 cups water
2 onions, sliced
2 bay leaves
1 teaspoon peppercorns
¼ cup sugar
2 tablespoons lard

1. Rub meat with cut surface of garlic, then with salt and pepper. Put meat and garlic into a deep casserole having a cover.
2. Heat the vinegar, water, onions, bay leaves, peppercorns, and sugar just until boiling; pour over meat and allow to cool. Cover and refrigerate 4 days, turning meat each day.
3. Remove meat; strain and reserve liquid.
4. Brown meat in heated lard in a Dutch oven, turning to brown evenly. Add half of the reserved liquid; cover and simmer 2 to 3 hours, or until meat is tender, adding additional liquid as needed. Slice meat; serve with Potato Dumplings, and, if desired, Gingersnap Gravy (page 28).

6 to 8 servings

Gingersnap Gravy: Stir ¾ cup crushed gingersnaps and 1 tablespoon sugar into cooking liquid in Dutch oven. Simmer 10 minutes; stir occasionally.

Potato Dumplings (Kartoffelklösse)

    1 to 2 slices bread, cut in ½-inch cubes
    1 to 1½ tablespoons butter or margarine
    1 egg, well beaten
    6 potatoes, mashed or riced and cooled
    1 teaspoon salt
    ⅛ teaspoon white pepper
    ¼ cup cornstarch
    ⅔ to ¾ cup all-purpose flour

1. Brown bread cubes lightly on all sides in heated butter in a large skillet; set aside.
2. Whip egg into cooled mashed potatoes until fluffy. Stir in salt, pepper, and cornstarch. Mix in enough flour to make a soft dough.
3. Break off pieces of dough and shape into 1-inch balls. Poke one of the bread cubes into the center of each ball.
4. Drop dumplings into **boiling salted water** (2 quarts water and 2 teaspoons salt), only as many as will lie uncrowded one layer deep. Cook about 5 minutes, or until dumplings rise to surface. Using a slotted spoon, remove dumplings; drain over water a few seconds. Put into a heated serving dish. Serve with **melted butter.**

About 18 dumplings

Pastitsio, Budget Style

    1 pint (2 cups) Hamburger Mix (page 19)
    1 can (8 ounces) tomatoes
    ¼ teaspoon thyme
    1 box (7 or 8 ounces) elbow macaroni
    4 egg whites
    ½ cup margarine
    ½ cup all-purpose flour
    1 teaspoon salt
    ¼ teaspoon cinnamon
    1 quart milk or 1⅓ cups instant nonfat
        milk solids plus 3¾ cups water
    4 egg yolks, slightly beaten
    ¼ teaspoon cinnamon

1. In saucepan, combine Hamburger Mix, tomatoes, and thyme; heat thoroughly. Remove from heat.
2. Meanwhile, cook macaroni according to package directions. Drain and add egg whites. Combine with meat mixture. Pour into greased 13×9×2-inch pan or two greased 8×8×2-inch pans.
3. Melt margarine in a large saucepan over low heat. Blend in flour, salt, and ¼ teaspoon cinnamon. Cook, stirring constantly, until mixture bubbles up. Add milk slowly; continue stirring. When the mixture thickens, remove from heat. Cool slightly.
4. Stir a small amount of the sauce into the egg yolks. Add this mixture to the sauce, stirring rapidly. When the sauce is smooth, pour over meat combination. Sprinkle lightly with cinnamon.
5. Bake at 375°F 30 minutes, or until the topping is set when tested with a knife.

About 12 servings

Note: ½ cup crumbled feta cheese can be added to the meat mixture, and makes the Pastitsio more authentic, but removes the recipe from the budget category.

Brioche

    ½ cup butter
    ⅓ cup sugar
    ½ teaspoon salt
    ½ cup undiluted evaporated milk
    1 package active dry yeast
    ¼ cup warm water
    1 egg yolk
    2 eggs
    3¼ cups all-purpose flour
    1 egg white; unbeaten
    1 tablespoon sugar

1. Cream the butter with the ⅓ cup sugar and salt in a large bowl. Beat in the evaporated milk.
2. Soften yeast in the warm water.
3. Beat egg yolk with the eggs until thick and piled softly. Gradually add to the creamed mixture, beating constantly until fluffy. Blend in the yeast.

4. Add the flour, about ½ cup at a time, beating thoroughly after each addition. Cover; let rise in a warm place until doubled, about 2 hours.

5. Stir down and beat thoroughly. Cover tightly with moisture-vaporproof material and refrigerate overnight.

6. Remove from refrigerator and stir down the dough. Turn onto a lightly floured surface and divide into two portions, one using about three fourths of the dough, the other about one fourth.

7. Cut each portion into 16 equal pieces. Roll each piece into a smooth ball. Place each large ball in a well-greased muffin-pan well (2¾ × 1¼ inches). Make a deep indentation with finger in center of each large ball; then moisten each depression slightly with cold water. Press a small ball into each depression.

8. Cover; let rise again until more than doubled, about 1 hour.

9. Brush tops of rolls with a mixture of the egg white and 1 tablespoon sugar.

10. Bake at 375°F about 15 minutes, or until golden brown.

16 brioches

Penny-wise Pizza

- 1 package active dry yeast
- ¾ cup warm water
- 2¼ cups Multi-Purpose Baking Mix (page 15)
- 1 pint (2 cups) Hamburger Mix (page 19)
- 1 teaspoon oregano
- ¼ pound pasteurized process American cheese, sliced and cut in strips

1. Dissolve the yeast in warm water.

2. Turn Baking Mix into a mixing bowl, add yeast, and beat vigorously.

3. Turn dough onto floured surface; knead with fingertips about 20 times, or until smooth. Allow dough to "rest" a few minutes after kneading.

4. Divide dough into 4 pieces. Roll each into a very thin circle 9 inches across, being careful not to tear dough. Place on ungreased baking sheets or pie pans.

5. Combine Hamburger Mix and oregano; heat thoroughly. Divide onto the 4 rounds (about ½ cup of Hamburger Mix to each), and spread it evenly over the dough.

6. Bake at 425°F 15 to 20 minutes, or until crust is brown. Remove from oven and arrange cheese strips on top.

7. Turn oven control to 350°F. Return pizzas to oven just long enough to melt the cheese.

4 (9-inch) pizzas

Liver Pâté Exceptionale

Pâté:
- 1 pound onions, sliced
- 1 clove garlic, finely minced
- ¼ cup rendered chicken fat or shortening
- 1 pound chicken livers, coarsely diced
- 1 teaspoon salt
- Few grains freshly ground black pepper

Sauce:
- 1¼ cups olive or vegetable oil
- ¾ cup horseradish mustard
- ¼ cup vinegar
- ½ cup finely diced celery
- ½ cup finely diced onion
- ¼ cup snipped parsley
- 1 tablespoon paprika
- 1 teaspoon salt
- ½ teaspoon freshly ground black pepper

1. For pâté, add the onions and garlic to hot chicken fat in a skillet. Cook, stirring occasionally, until onion is golden.

2. Add chicken livers, salt, and pepper to mixture in skillet. Cook the livers until cooked through, but not browned.

3. Put the onion-liver mixture through a food chopper; turn into a bowl and whip to a smooth paste with rotary beater. If pâté is too thick, add **chicken broth** until of desired consistency.

4. For sauce, combine the oil in a bowl with remaining ingredients; mix well. Serve with the liver pâté.

2 cups pâté and 3 cups sauce

Low-cost Lasagne

1 pound lasagne noodles
2 pints Hamburger Mix (page 19)
1 can (15 ounces) tomato sauce
1 teaspoon oregano
2 cups (1 pound) creamed cottage cheese
1 cup dairy sour half-and-half or sour cream substitute (page 26)
1 egg
2 tablespoons chopped parsley
½ teaspoon salt
  Dash pepper
12 slices pasteurized process American cheese
  Grated Parmesan cheese (optional)

1. Boil lasagne noodles according to package directions until slightly tender.
2. Heat Hamburger Mix with tomato sauce and oregano until heated through.
3. In large bowl, combine cottage cheese, sour half-and-half, egg, chopped parsley, salt and pepper.
4. In a greased 13×9×2-inch baking pan, spread 1 cup of the hamburger sauce; add ⅓ of the lasagne noodles in an even layer; cover with a layer of the cottage cheese mixture, and arrange 6 slices process cheese evenly. Repeat layers twice (except for cheese slices), ending with meat sauce on top. Sprinkle with Parmesan cheese, if desired.
5. Bake at 350°F 30 minutes, or until bubbly. Let stand 10 minutes before serving; cut into squares and serve hot.

16 servings

Stroganoff, Economy Class

1½ pounds beef round or chuck steak
2 cups hot water
2 medium onions, sliced
2 tablespoons oil or shortening
½ cup (4-ounce can) drained mushroom stems and pieces
2 tablespoons ketchup or tomato paste
3 beef bouillon cubes
1 teaspoon prepared or ½ teaspoon dry mustard
½ teaspoon salt
2 tablespoons flour
½ cup cold water
½ cup dairy sour cream or sour cream substitute (page 26)

1. Cut beef into thin strips and put into a saucepot. Add hot water, cover, and simmer 1 to 1½ hours, or until tender.
2. In a large fry pan, sauté onions in oil until tender.
3. Add meat with broth, mushrooms, ketchup, bouillon cubes, mustard, and salt to onions. Cover; simmer 15 minutes.
4. Combine flour with cold water. Slowly stir into meat mixture. Cook, stirring constantly, until mixture comes to a boil.
5. Remove pan from heat; stir in sour cream. Stir until mixture is smooth. Return to low heat and cook only until heated through. Serve with **rice** or **noodles**.

6 servings

Polenta with Meat Sauce

Mush:
1 cup enriched cornmeal
1 teaspoon salt
2 cups milk
2 cups boiling water

Meat Sauce:
½ cup chopped onion
½ cup chopped celery
2 tablespoons shortening
1 pound ground beef
1 can (16 ounces) whole tomatoes, chopped and drained
1 can (8 ounces) tomato sauce
1 can (6 ounces) tomato paste
1 can (8¾ ounces) whole kernel corn, drained
1 teaspoon salt
¼ teaspoon pepper

1. For mush, combine cornmeal, salt, and milk; add slowly to boiling water, stirring constantly until slightly thickened; cover. Continue cooking over low heat about 10 minutes, stirring occasionally. Pour into ungreased 8-inch square pan. Chill until firmly set, several hours or overnight.
2. For meat sauce, lightly sauté onion and celery in shortening in large skillet. Add ground beef and brown well; drain. Stir in remaining ingredients.
3. Cut chilled cornmeal mush into 6 pieces. Arrange in an ungreased 11×7×3-inch baking pan. Spoon meat sauce over and around mush pieces.
4. Bake in a 400°F oven about 25 minutes, or until heated through.

6 servings

BUDGETING FOR ONE OR TWO

Singles and couples have problems of their own when it comes to food budgeting. "Economy" sizes are usually jumbo sizes, and most recipes for economy meat cuts serve a crowd.

But the basic budgeting techniques still apply, and the same nutrient needs must be met. While there may not be the incentive for a live-aloner or twosome to plan meals as carefully as a mother with a growing family, the stakes are still the same—good nutrition for good health.

To make sure you include all the basics in your meal plans, see the chart on page 11.

Planning does pay off, for one as much as for a family. Not only does it assure that all Basic Four bases will be covered; it will help you to make better use of leftovers. You can give more interest to meals by advance-planning some variations for the food you prepare, rather than merely reheating it the second time around.

PLANNING FOR THE COUPLE

There is a false report circulating that two can live as cheaply as one. Nowhere is its falsehood more transparent than at the food store. However, with careful shopping, two can live for something less than twice the expense of one.

Planning meals for a couple is similar to planning for a family, in that meals should be based on foods you like best as well as nutrient needs. And you still must consider the limitations of your budget, time schedule, and cooking ability. Keeping all that in

mind, work out menus for a week. Or try the ones on page 32 as a guide.

When first cooking for a twosome, either as a bride, roommate, or "empty nester," there are some adjustments to be made. If you're used to cooking in family-sized quantities, you'll find yourself overcooking for a while.

The retired couple may also need to find lower calorie dishes than were customary when a growing family gathered at the table. For them, less cooking may prove to be a happy answer. Fresh fruits and vegetables, in salad bowls and dessert trays, not only mean less work and lower calories, but fewer leftovers, as well.

Not that you'll want to give up your old favorite family recipes. Prepare them from time to time in full quantity, and freeze leftovers in several small-meal packets to enjoy later on.

BATCHING IT

For the person newly on his own, the experience of eating alone takes some getting used to. Eating is basically a social experience, so it pays to work at making mealtimes pleasant, even when setting the table for one.

Turn on the radio or television, or prop up a book. Really sit down and enjoy the meal, rather than eating on the run.

Plan your meals for a whole week, and see how they stack up nutritionally (check the chart on page 11). Then draw up a shopping list and play the budget game; see what bargains you can find in small quantities at the store.

Or try our planned menus for a week. Go through them, before going to the store, to adapt them to your own personal tastes; make substitutions where needed. Perhaps you'd like to include more convenience foods, and you will want to take advantage of advertised specials.

Correct the shopping list to conform to your changes, add any staples (flour, sugar, and other frequently used pantry items), and you'll be well armed for a foray into the marketplace.

The couple who tested these menus found it harder to stay within the low-budget range suggested by the U.S. Department of Agriculture than did the family of five who tested their weekly plans (page 83). But the couple needed to buy staples less frequently, which helped to cut their expenses. And shopping with a list reduced impulse buying.

WEEK'S MENUS FOR A TWOSOME OR LIVE-ALONER

 Sunday

Breakfast
Grapefruit Half, or Melon in season
Poached Egg
Toasted English Muffin   Jelly
Coffee or Milk

Dinner
Roast Pork with Pan Gravy
Mashed Potato   Buttered Lima Beans
Lettuce Wedge with Onion French
    Dressing (page 24)
Purchased Cupcake
Tea or Milk

Snack
Cheese and Crackers
Fruit-Topped Ice-Milk Sundae

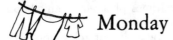 Monday

Breakfast
Orange Juice
French Toast   Homemade Syrup
Coffee or Milk

Lunch
Cheese Sandwich   Carrot Sticks
Cupcake   Milk

Dinner
Fish Sticks with Tartar Sauce
Baked Potato
Fruit Mold Salad in Lettuce Cup
Chilled Melon or Broiled Grapefruit Half
    with Honey Topping
Coffee or Milk

 Tuesday

Breakfast
Tomato Juice   Packaged Cereal
Coffee or Milk

Lunch
Cottage Cheese   Celery Sticks
Fruit Mold Salad
Wheat Toast   Milk

Dinner
Pork, Macaroni, and Vegetable Casserole
    (page 40—use half recipe)
Tossed Green Salad with Onion French
    Dressing (page 24)
Hot Biscuits (page 16)   Jelly
Tea or Milk

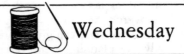 Wednesday

Breakfast
Stewed Prunes in Orange Juice
Sunnyside Egg   Toast
Coffee or Milk

Lunch
Process Cheese Strips Wrapped in
    Lunchmeat
Toasted English Muffin
Fresh Fruit   Milk

Dinner
Twosome Meat Loaf (page 34)
Cottage Cheese in Lettuce Cup
Fruit Mold Square with Whipped Topping
Coffee or Milk

Eggs Florentine à l'Orange;
Cottage Cheese Rolls;
Grapefruit Spritzer

Thursday

Breakfast

>Apple Sauce with Brown Sugar Topping or
>   Melon, in season
>Cereal   Coffee or Milk

Lunch

>Canned Sardines   Crackers
>Lettuce Wedge with Dressing
>Cookies   Milk

Dinner

>Scrambled Eggs in Salami Cups (page 34)
>Buttered Carrots
>Tossed Green Salad
>Bread   Butter
>Ice Milk with Fresh Fruit Topping
>Tea or Milk

Friday

Breakfast

>Grapefruit Juice   Cereal with Raisins
>Toast Topped with Cinnamon-Sugar
>   Mixture
>Coffee or Milk

Lunch

>Peanut Butter Sandwich
>Fresh Fruit   Milk

Dinner

>Pan-Fried Ham Slice with Canned Crushed
>   Pineapple Topping
>Boiled Potato   Buttered Green Beans
>Ice Milk Shake

Saturday

Breakfast

>Grapefruit Juice
>Eggs Benedict (toasted English muffin half
>   topped with leftover ham slice, poached
>   egg, and homemade or bottled
>   hollandaise sauce)
>Extra English Muffin, if desired
>Coffee or Milk

Lunch

>Onion Soup

Green Pepper Halves (parboiled) Baked
   with a Filling of Hamburger Mix (page
   19)
Crackers
Crushed Pineapple   Milk

Dinner

>Baked Chicken Drumsticks
>Baked Sweet Potato
>Marinated Green Bean Salad
>Fresh Fruit   Tea or Milk

SHOPPING LIST

Bakery

Cupcakes
English muffins
Whole wheat bread

Canned Foods

Fruits
>Applesauce
>Crushed pineapple
>Mixed fruit for salad

Juices
>Grapefruit
>Tomato

Vegetables
>Lima beans
>Green beans

Dairy Foods and Eggs

Butter or margarine
Cheddar or American cheese
Cottage cheese
Eggs
Milk
Parmesan cheese
Sour cream

Choose-a-Partner Tuna Casserole

Frozen Foods

Fish sticks
Ice milk
Orange juice

Meat, Poultry, and Fish

Chicken drumsticks
Ground beef
Pork roast
Ham slice
Salami

Packaged Foods

Breakfast cereals
Crackers
Dried prunes
Dry onion soup mix
Fruit-flavored gelatin
Raisins

Produce

Fruits
    Grapefruit
    Selection of 2 or 3 other fruits in
      season
Vegetables
    Carrots
    Celery
    Green peppers
    Lettuce
    Onions
    Sweet potatoes
    White potatoes

Scrambled Eggs in Salami Cups

2 slices salami
  Butter or margarine
3 eggs
¼ teaspoon salt
  Few grains pepper
¼ teaspoon prepared mustard
3 tablespoons milk, dairy sour cream, or
  sour cream substitute (page 26)

1. Panfry salami slices in a small amount of butter; the edges will cup up. Remove to serving dish and keep warm.
2. Combine eggs in a bowl with salt, pepper, mustard, and milk, mixing with a fork only until blended.
3. Add about 1 tablespoon more butter to skillet. Heat until melted and hot enough to sizzle when a drop of water is added.
4. Pour in egg mixture; cook over low heat, lifting egg mixture from sides and bottom as it thickens; do not stir. Cook until done as desired.
5. Spoon scrambled eggs into salami cups.

2 servings

Twosome Meat Loaf

½ pound lean ground beef
½ teaspoon salt
  Few grains pepper
⅛ teaspoon dry mustard
¼ teaspoon onion powder
1 egg, beaten
¼ cup uncooked oats
2 tablespoons sweet pickle liquid (or
  water)
1 tablespoon ketchup
1 tablespoon sweet pickle liquid (or
  water)
1 teaspoon brown sugar

1. In a bowl lightly mix the ground beef with a blend of salt, pepper, dry mustard, and onion powder, the beaten egg, oats, and 2 tablespoons pickle liquid.
2. Shape into 2 loaves and put into a shallow baking pan. Spoon a mixture of remaining ingredients over loaves.
3. Bake at 350°F 30 to 35 minutes.

2 servings

LEFTOVERS

There are times when deception is not only permitted, it's encouraged. When you cook leftovers is one of those times.

As with pudding, the test of the leftover dish is in the tasting. If it comes across as a creative, delectable dish, and nobody recognizes it as arriving the second time around, you know you have a winner.

You are most apt to enjoy that sort of success when the leftover is really a "planned-over"—the initial purchase was made with this encore dish in mind.

A repertoire of later-day meals from large cuts of meat is a must for the budget cook.

But in addition to those major, most obvious leftovers are the dibs and dabs that work their way to the back of the refrigerator. Those are the ones that plague the budgeter with decisions of how to cope.

Our chart will suggest uses for both kinds of remnants—big and small. Make an extra effort to use all of everything. Perhaps there is no free lunch, but you can come close by turning small leftovers into sandwich fillings.

But there is a place to draw the line. If converting a small leftover into a recipe means tying up several other ingredients into something that may produce still more leftovers, you may be better advised to toss out the first leftover, and be done with it. And consider why it became a leftover—perhaps the family didn't relish it the first time around.

To see how long it's safe to store food in the refrigerator or freezer, check the charts on pages 89 and 90.

THE ABC OF LEFTOVERS

Bacon Crumble to top salads, soups, sandwiches, creamed vegetables, scrambled eggs.

Bacon fat Store covered in refrigerator. Use within 2 weeks for frying.

Bread *Day old:* Toast or French toast. When drier (but not moldy) cut into cubes and use for bread pudding or oven-toast for croutons or bread stuffing. Oven-toast whole slices to crush for bread crumbs.

Quick breads, such as cornbread, biscuits, and muffins: Split and toast.

Cereal (cooked) Add to ground meat to replace bread crumbs in meat-loaf mixtures. Or spread in rectangular pan while still warm, chill, cut into squares, and pan-fry. Serve with syrup.

Cheese Grate or chop; store in airtight bags in freezer to use as casserole toppings or in sandwich spreads. Can be grated even if dried out but not moldy.

Chicken or turkey	Add to salad or sandwich makings. Serve creamed over toast. Make pie or casserole. Use bones for soup.
Eggs	*Hard-cooked:* Chop and use in salads and sandwiches.
	White only: Use for meringues, angel cake or white cake, fluffy hard sauce, divinity candy, white icings, macaroons. Use to dip food before breading and to brush pie shells before baking.
	Yolk only: Baked custard, cooked custard, Bavarian cream, custard filling, scrambled, mayonnaise or hollandaise sauce, yellow cake. Drop unbroken yolks into simmering water and cook until firm; chop or rice for use in salads, sandwiches, and garnish.
Fish	Use in salads and soufflés. Mash with filling for deviled eggs.
Fruit	Use in crisps and cobblers. Combine with ice cream for dessert.
	Juice: Substitute for water in gelatin recipes. Use in cocktails and combine with other juices for beverages. Baste ham or pot roast. Substitute for water in cooking dried fruits. Use in salad dressings.
Gravy	Reheat with chopped leftover meat; serve over rice, noodles, or toast.
Jelly	Combine with just enough boiling water to make sauce to pour over pudding. Stir into confectioners' sugar frosting for cookies and coffeecake.
Meats	Use in croquettes, salads, soufflés, casseroles, sandwich fillings, creamed on toast or pasta, in pies, stuffed peppers, stew, and soup.
Pickle juice	Substitute for vinegar in salad dressing. Use to pickle fresh onions or beets.
Potatoes	*Boiled:* Potatoes au gratin, potato salad, creamed potatoes, sautéed potatoes, and in meat pies.
	Mashed: Baked, sautéed potato dumplings, or cakes. Put through pastry tube and oven-brown for meat tray garnish.
Rice	Add to soups and casseroles. Serve cold with cinnamon and sugar or fruit, or with sugar and cream topping, for dessert. Make rice pudding.
Sausage, cooked	Add to sandwich mixtures, soup, casserole combinations, and antipasto tray.
Soup	Add to gravy or other sauce having similar base.
Vegetables	Add to soup, soufflé, use to make stock, add to omelets, in meat pies, marinate in salad dressing, and prepare herbed vegetable platter or antipasto tray.

Glazed Ham Loaf

3 cups ground cooked ham or smoked pork shoulder
¾ cup uncooked oats
2 eggs, slightly beaten
½ cup milk
⅔ cup packed brown sugar
2 tablespoons flour
1 teaspoon dry mustard
⅛ teaspoon ground cloves
⅔ cup apricot nectar or syrup drained from canned fruit such as apricots, peaches, or pears
2 tablespoons vinegar

1. Combine ground ham, oats, eggs, and milk in bowl, mixing until thoroughly blended.
2. Shape into loaf in a 9×5×3-inch loaf pan.

3. Bake in 325°F oven 1 hour. Pour excess fat from pan.

4. Blend brown sugar, flour, dry mustard, and cloves in a saucepan. Add nectar and vinegar; stir and cook over low heat until thickened. Pour over ham loaf and continue baking 20 minutes.

8 servings

Ham 'n' Taters

    4 medium potatoes
    2 tablespoons shortening
    2 cups cubed cooked ham or smoked pork
        shoulder
    1 cup milk

1. Pare and cut potatoes into ½-inch cubes. Pat dry.

2. Melt shortening in skillet. Add potato cubes; stir and fry until cubes are lightly browned, 5 to 10 minutes.

3. Add meat and milk; stir to blend.

4. Cover and cook slowly about 5 minutes. Uncover and continue cooking until all the milk is absorbed. Season as desired.

About 4 servings

Ham-Bean Soup

    2 quarts water
    1 pound (about 2 cups) dried Great
        Northern or pea beans
    3 tablespoons butter
    2 cups finely chopped onion
    ½ cup finely chopped celery
    2 teaspoons finely chopped garlic
    3 cans (about 10 ounces each) condensed
        chicken broth
      Water
    1 ham shank (about 4 pounds) or 2 ham
        hocks (about 1½ pounds)
    1 can (about 16 ounces) tomatoes or 4 to 6
        medium-sized firm ripe tomatoes,
        peeled and chopped
    2 whole cloves
    1 bay leaf
    ¼ teaspoon freshly ground black pepper
    2 cups shredded Cheddar cheese (about 8
        ounces)

1. Bring water to boiling in a 6-quart saucepot. Add beans gradually to water so that boiling continues. Boil 2 minutes. Remove from heat and set aside 1 hour.

2. Drain beans, reserving liquid. Return beans to saucepot along with 4 cups of cooking liquid.

3. Melt butter in a large skillet. Add onion, celery, and garlic; cook 5 minutes, stirring occasionally. Turn contents of skillet into saucepot.

4. Combine chicken broth with enough water to make 6 cups. Pour into saucepot.

5. Peel skin from ham shank and cut off excess fat. Add shank and skin to saucepot along with tomatoes, cloves, bay leaf, and pepper. Bring to boiling, reduce heat, and simmer 2 to 2½ hours, or until ham is tender.

6. Remove ham shank and skin; cool. Transfer soup to a large bowl; remove bay leaf and cloves. Cut meat into pieces and return to soup. Refrigerate, then skim off fat.

7. Transfer soup to saucepot and bring to simmer. Add cheese and stir until melted.

About 4 quarts soup

Note: Soup may be stored in the refrigerator and reheated, or cooled and poured into freezer containers and frozen. Thaw and reheat over low heat.

Ham Balls in Sour Cream Sauce

    ¼ cup chopped onion
    ¼ cup shortening
    3 cups ground cooked ham or smoked
        pork shoulder
    ¼ teaspoon pepper
    1 egg, slightly beaten
    2 tablespoons flour
    ¾ cup water
    ¼ teaspoon dill seed
    ¼ teaspoon marjoram
    1 cup dairy sour cream or sour cream
        substitute (page 26)

1. Cook onion in shortening in a skillet. Remove onion and combine with ham, pepper, and egg in a mixing bowl.

2. Shape mixture into 2-inch balls and brown evenly on all sides in hot shortening. Remove balls from skillet and keep hot while making sauce.

3. Combine flour with remaining shortening in skillet. Add water, dill seed, and marjoram. Stir and cook until thickened, reduce heat, and cook 3 minutes.

4. Stir in sour cream and heat thoroughly. Pour over ham balls on a platter and serve.

4 or 5 servings

Turkey Fondue Sandwiches

8 slices cooked turkey, ¼ inch thick
4 slices pasteurized process American cheese
8 slices sandwich bread
4 eggs
2 cups milk
½ teaspoon salt
Paprika

1. Butter a 9-inch square glass baking dish. Make four turkey and cheese sandwiches. Place sandwiches in single layer in baking dish.
2. Beat eggs until light and frothy. Add milk and salt. Pour over sandwiches. Sprinkle top with paprika.
3. Bake at 325°F 40 to 45 minutes.

4 sandwiches

Turkey Soufflé

½ cup shredded Swiss cheese (about 2 ounces)
1 can (about 10 ounces) condensed cream of chicken soup
1 teaspoon chopped green onion
1 teaspoon chopped parsley
¼ teaspoon dry mustard
⅛ teaspoon pepper
6 eggs
1 cup diced cooked turkey

1. Combine Swiss cheese, soup, onion, parsley, mustard, and pepper in a large saucepan. Place over very low heat and stir until cheese just melts.

2. Separate eggs and beat in egg yolks one at a time. Stir in turkey.
3. Beat egg whites until stiff but not dry. Fold into cheese mixture.
4. Pour into a well-buttered 2-quart soufflé dish.
5. Bake at 375°F about 30 minutes. Serve at once.

About 5 servings

Meat-Cottage Cheese Mold

1 envelope unflavored gelatin
½ cup cold water
1 chicken bouillon cube
½ cup water
1½ cups creamed cottage cheese
1 cup minced cooked meat, such as beef, ham, chicken, turkey, or tongue
½ cup chopped red and/or green pepper
¼ teaspoon salt
⅛ teaspoon pepper
Salad greens

1. Soften gelatin in ½ cup cold water in a saucepan; add bouillon cube and stir over low heat until gelatin and bouillon cube are dissolved.
2. Remove from heat, add ½ cup water and cottage cheese, and beat thoroughly. Chill until slightly thickened.
3. Mix meat, chopped pepper, salt, and pepper into thickened gelatin. Turn into a 1-quart mold or 4 individual 8-ounce molds. Chill until set.
4. Unmold salad and garnish with salad greens. Serve with desired dressing.

4 to 6 servings

Hearty Poultry Pie

4 cups Pie Crust Mix (page 18)
5 to 6 tablespoons cold water, or just enough to hold pastry together
3 cups cubed cooked chicken or turkey
1 can (17 ounces) cream-style corn
3 cups cooked rice
1 pound sliced bacon, cut in 1-inch pieces and fried
½ teaspoon salt
¼ teaspoon pepper
¼ cup chicken broth or water

1. Prepare pie crust and divide into halves. Roll out one half, line a deep 10-inch pie plate or 2½-quart casserole with pastry, and flute edges high.
2. Layer the chicken cubes, corn, rice, and bacon

until all ingredients are used. Mixture will be quite high above edge of pie plate.

3. Add salt and pepper to broth and pour evenly over mixture.

4. Roll out top pastry, cutting slits for steam to escape; put pastry in place. Cut extra pastry into fancy shapes and decorate top of pie.

5. Bake at 375°F 1 hour, or until browned and bubbly.

8 to 12 servings

Turkey Soup

- 1 turkey carcass
- 3 stalks celery with tops, coarsely chopped
- 1 onion, sliced
- 1 tablespoon salt
- 1 bay leaf
- 3 quarts water
- 1 package (1¾ ounces) dry chicken noodle soup mix

1. Simmer turkey carcass, celery, onion, salt, and bay leaf in water in a covered saucepot about 2 hours. Turn turkey if necessary during cooking. Remove carcass.

2. Strip meat from bones and add to broth. Bring soup to a boil and add soup mix. Simmer about 10 minutes. This soup is even better if made the day before it is served.

About 13 cups soup

Note: Small amounts of cooked vegetables such as peas, corn, or carrots may be added with the soup mix.

Scalloped Turkey

- ½ cup chopped celery
- ¼ cup chopped green pepper
- 3 tablespoons butter or margarine
- 2 tablespoons flour
- ¼ teaspoon salt
- 1½ cups milk
- 2 cups diced cooked turkey
- 1 tablespoon chopped pimento
- 2 cups lightly crushed potato chips

1. Sauté celery and green pepper in 1 tablespoon butter in a saucepan. Remove vegetables from pan.

2. Melt remaining butter in saucepan. Blend in flour and salt.

3. Gradually add milk, stirring constantly; cook until mixture thickens. Add turkey, celery, green pepper, and pimento.

4. Put about 1½ cups crushed potato chips in

bottom of a buttered 1- to 1½-quart baking dish; add turkey mixture. Sprinkle remaining chips on top.

5. Heat in a 350°F oven 30 to 40 minutes, or until sauce bubbles.

4 servings

Creamy Seasoned Turkey

- 1 can (about 10 ounces) condensed cream of chicken soup
- 1 egg, slightly beaten
- ¼ cup milk
- 3 cups cubed cooked turkey
- 1 can (2 ounces) mushrooms
- 2 tablespoons chopped pimento
- ¼ teaspoon celery salt
- ¼ teaspoon black pepper
- ⅛ teaspoon chili powder
  cup shredded sharp Cheddar cheese (about 4 ounces)
- 3 cups cooked rice

1. Blend and heat soup, egg, and milk in a saucepan.

2. Add all remaining ingredients except rice and mix well. Heat. Serve turkey mixture over hot rice.

About 6 servings

Beef-Curry Skillet Dish

    1 tablespoon fat
    1 cup chopped onion
    2 tablespoons flour
    1 to 2 teaspoons curry powder
    2 teaspoons salt
    1 cup water
 2½ cups minced cooked beef
    2 cups (about 2 large) potatoes, diced
    1 can (8 ounces) tomatoes

1. In a heavy kettle, melt fat and sauté onion until tender, about 5 minutes.
2. Sprinkle with flour, curry powder, and salt; stir until well blended.
3. Gradually stir in water.
4. Add cooked beef and diced potatoes. Cover and simmer, stirring occasionally, 20 minutes, or until potatoes are tender.
5. Mix in tomatoes and cook a few minutes longer, or until heated through.

4 to 6 servings

Turkey Mushroom Bake

    1 cup sliced mushrooms
    ½ cup chopped onion
    ¼ cup butter or margarine
    ¼ cup flour
    2 bouillon cubes
    2 cups boiling water
    1 cup milk
    1 teaspoon salt
    ¼ teaspoon poultry seasoning
    ⅛ teaspoon pepper
    2 packages (10 ounces each) frozen
        broccoli spears, cooked and drained
   10 slices cooked turkey
    ½ cup shredded Cheddar cheese (about 2
        ounces)

1. Brown mushrooms and onion in butter. Stir in flour. Cook until bubbly.
2. Dissolve bouillon cubes in boiling water. Add bouillon, milk, and seasonings to mushroom-onion mixture. Cook, stirring constantly, until mixture boils.
3. Place a layer of cooked broccoli in a buttered 13×9×2-inch baking dish. Cover with three-fourths of mushroom sauce.
4. Place turkey slices in a layer over broccoli and sauce. Cover turkey slices with remaining sauce. Sprinkle cheese on top.
5. Bake at 400°F about 15 minutes, or until cheese melts.

8 to 10 servings

Pork, Macaroni, and Vegetable Casserole

    2 cups cubed cooked pork roast
    ¼ cup shortening
    2 cups chopped celery
    1 cup chopped onion
    ½ cup macaroni (about 2¼ cups cooked)
    1 cup cooked lima beans
    1 cup tomato juice
    2 tablespoons ketchup
    2 teaspoons salt
    ¼ teaspoon pepper

1. Brown cubed cooked pork in shortening in a large skillet. Add celery and onion and cook over low heat until tender, about 10 minutes.
2. Cook macaroni in boiling salted water, following package directions; drain. Add to pork mixture along with remaining ingredients.
3. Transfer to greased baking dish.
4. Cover and bake at 350°F for 20 to 30 minutes, or until bubbly.

4 to 6 servings

BUDGET-SAVING RECIPES

SOUPS AND STEWS

A hallmark of the accomplished chef is the ever-simmering stockpot catching remnants of meat and vegetables to provide *soup du jour* or the base for a stew.

The soup kettle can perform the same service in the home. Bones from roast meat, or the carcass of a bird, can be transformed into a rich soup. Add a few vegetables, perhaps leftovers themselves, and you have the makings of a satisfying first course or a lunch-in-one dish.

Homemade soups and stews are economical, but require fairly generous amounts of time, so they are best suited to the life of a stay-at-home. However, with a slow-cooking pot, even the office worker can start something cooking before leaving home and enjoy it after hours.

Borsch

    1 can (16 ounces) whole beets
  ¼ cup sugar
  ¾ teaspoon salt
  5 tablespoons lemon juice
  1 egg, well beaten

1. Drain contents of can of beets, reserving liquid in a 1-quart measuring cup. Put beets through food mill (or finely chop beets in an electric blender, adding about ½ cup of the reserved liquid to the blender container). Add beet pulp to liquid in measuring cup and add water to make 1 quart.

2. Heat beet-water mixture, sugar, salt, and lemon juice to boiling in a saucepan, stirring occasionally.

3. Remove from heat and gradually add ¾ cup of the hot mixture to beaten egg, stirring constantly; stir into beet mixture in saucepan. Return to heat; cook, stirring, until simmering (do not boil).

4. Serve hot or cold, topped with **dairy sour cream.**

About 1 quart soup

Dutch-Style Chowder

    4 slices bacon, diced
  ⅓ cup chopped onion
  1 can (about 10 ounces) condensed cream of chicken soup
  1 can (about 10 ounces) condensed chicken-vegetable soup
  1 soup can milk
  1 soup can water
  1 cup drained canned whole kernel corn
  2 tablespoons snipped parsley

1. Cook bacon in a saucepan until crisp. Remove from pan to absorbent paper.

2. Pour off all except 1 tablespoon fat from pan. Add onion and cook until tender.

3. Stir in the soups, milk, water, and corn. Heat thoroughly, stirring frequently.

4. Garnish chowder with bacon and parsley.

About 6 servings

Frankfurter-Chicken Cream Soup

2 tablespoons butter
1 medium-sized onion, cut in ¼-inch slices
5 frankfurters, cut in ¼-inch slices
1 can (about 10 ounces) condensed cream of chicken soup
1 soup can water
1 soup can milk
2 chicken bouillon cubes
¼ teaspoon ground mace
½ teaspoon grated lemon peel

1. Heat butter in a saucepan. Add onion and frankfurter slices. Cook until onion is transparent, occasionally moving and turning with a spoon.
2. Stir in the soup, then the water and milk, blending thoroughly after each addition.
3. Add bouillon cubes, stirring occasionally until completely dissolved. Stir in the mace and lemon peel and heat thoroughly (do not boil). Garnish with minced parsley.

About 6 servings

Cabbage Soup

1 pound cross-cut beef shanks
2 or 3 marrow bones
1 cup chopped onion
2 quarts water
1 small head cabbage, shredded
3 tablespoons salt
3 tablespoons sugar
½ cup lemon juice
1 tablespoon rendered chicken fat or shortening
2 tablespoons flour
Snipped parsley

1. Put meat, bones, and onion into a large, heavy saucepot. Add water and bring to boiling; remove foam. Cover and simmer about 1½ hours, or until meat is tender. Remove bones and cut meat into small pieces; return meat to soup.
2. Meanwhile, sprinkle cabbage with salt and let stand while soup is cooking. Pour boiling water over cabbage and drain thoroughly.
3. Add drained cabbage to soup when meat is tender. Cook, uncovered, over low heat about 45 minutes. Add sugar and lemon juice; cook 15 minutes longer.
4. Meanwhile, melt fat in a skillet; add flour. Stir over medium heat until flour becomes a deep brown. Gradually add some of the soup, stirring until smooth. Bring to boiling; cook 2 minutes, stirring constantly. Slowly pour flour mixture into soup, stirring constantly to prevent lumping.
5. Add more salt or sugar to taste, if desired. Pour into individual serving bowls; sprinkle with parsley.

About 3 quarts soup

Beef Soup

1½ pounds beef for stew
1 soup bone
1½ to 2 teaspoons salt
½ teaspoon pepper
2 bay leaves
4 medium-sized carrots, pared and sliced
1 cup chopped cabbage
1 cup chopped celery
½ cup chopped onion
1 can (15 ounces) Italian-style tomatoes
1 tablespoon Worcestershire sauce
1 beef bouillon cube
Pinch oregano (or other herb desired)

1. Put meat and soup bone in a heavy 3-quart kettle; cover with cold water (about 4 cups). Add salt, pepper, and bay leaves. Bring rapidly to boiling. Reduce heat. Add carrots, cabbage, celery, and onion; cover and simmer until meat is tender, about 2½ hours.
2. Remove and discard bone and bay leaves. Cut meat into bite-sized pieces and return to soup. Mix in tomatoes, Worcestershire sauce, bouillon cube, and oregano. Cover and simmer 30 minutes.

6 servings

Plantation Soup

3 cups beef broth
2 carrots, pared and chopped
2 stalks celery, chopped
2 small onions, chopped
3 tablespoons flour
6 tablespoons butter or margarine
3 cups milk
½ cup finely shredded Cheddar cheese (about 2 ounces)

1. Combine beef broth, carrots, celery, and onions in a saucepan. Bring to boiling; reduce heat and simmer, covered, 30 minutes, or until vegetables are very tender. Strain; set the broth aside.
2. Blend the flour into hot butter in a saucepan. Cook until bubbly, stirring constantly. Remove

from heat. Gradually add the milk, stirring constantly. Bring rapidly to boiling and boil 1 to 2 minutes, continuing to stir.

.3. Combine the strained broth with white sauce. Simmer, covered, about 20 minutes. When ready to serve, stir the cheese into the hot soup.

6 to 8 servings

Peanut Butter Soup

¼ cup finely chopped onion
⅓ cup finely chopped celery
2 tablespoons butter or margarine
1 tablespoon flour
2 cups milk
¾ cup chicken broth (dissolve 1 chicken bouillon cube in ¾ cup boiling water)
½ cup smooth peanut butter
¼ teaspoon salt

1. Cook the onion and celery in hot butter in a saucepan about 5 minutes, stirring occasionally. Blend in the flour and heat until mixture bubbles, stirring constantly.
2. Add milk and broth gradually, stirring constantly. Bring rapidly to boiling, stirring constantly. Cook 1 to 2 minutes to make white sauce.
3. Gradually stir white sauce into peanut butter until mixture is smooth. Return to saucepan. Stir in the salt and heat thoroughly. Serve garnished with **crumbled crisp-fried bacon**.

About 3 cups soup

Beef with Onions (Stifado)

2 pounds lean beef or pork, cut in 1½-inch pieces
2 tablespoons butter
2 tablespoons olive oil
4 pounds small white onions
4 firm ripe tomatoes, quartered
2 to 3 cloves garlic, minced
2 to 3 tablespoons wine vinegar
2 to 3 bay leaves

1. Brown meat on all sides in hot butter and oil in a large heavy saucepot.
2. Add remaining ingredients and then enough water to half cover ingredients in the pot. Season to taste with **salt** and **pepper**.
3. Bring to boiling, cover and simmer 1½ hours, or until meat is tender and liquid is reduced to a flavorful gravy.

4 to 6 servings

Szekely Goulash

1½ pounds boneless pork shoulder, cut in 1½-inch cubes
2 tablespoons flour
2 teaspoons paprika
1½ teaspoons salt
2 tablespoons fat
2 tablespoons finely chopped onion
1 can (27 ounces) sauerkraut, drained
½ teaspoon caraway seed
1½ cups dairy sour cream or sour cream substitute (see page 26)

1. Coat meat evenly with a mixture of flour, paprika, and salt.
2. Heat fat in a Dutch oven or saucepot. Add onion and cook until soft, stirring occasionally.
3. Brown meat evenly on all sides in the hot fat; add 3 tablespoons hot water. Cover and simmer 1 hour; stirring occasionally. Add small amounts of water as needed during cooking.
4. Mix sauerkraut and caraway seed with the meat; add 2 cups hot water. Cover and simmer 30 minutes, or until meat is tender.
5. Gradually add about 1½ cups of the cooking liquid to sour cream, blending well. Stir into mixture in Dutch oven. Stirring constantly, heat (do not boil) about 5 minutes. Serve in bowls; accompany with **boiled new potatoes**.

6 to 8 servings

"Boiled" Dinner

    4 pounds corned beef brisket
    ⅓ to ½ cup (about 1½ ounces) dry onion
       soup mix
    4 peppercorns
    1 clove garlic, minced
    1 bay leaf
    ¼ teaspoon rosemary, crushed
    3 cups water
    6 medium-sized potatoes, pared and
       quartered
    6 medium-sized carrots, pared and cut in
       1½-inch pieces
    ½ cup celery, cut in 1-inch pieces
    1 medium-sized head young green
       cabbage, cut in wedges

1. Put meat into a deep saucepot or Dutch oven
having a tight-fitting cover. Add soup mix, peppercorns, garlic, bay leaf, rosemary, and water. Cover,
bring to boiling, and simmer 3½ hours.
2. Add vegetables, placing cabbage on top of meat.
Cover and cook 1 hour, or until tender.
3. Remove vegetables and meat to a large heated
serving platter. If desired, thicken liquid in saucepot and serve in a gravy boat.

6 to 8 servings

cook the remaining vegetables separately in boiling
salted water until tender. Drain.
4. Turn contents of Dutch oven into a food mill set
over a large bowl. Return meat to the Dutch oven
and add the cooked onions, carrots, and turnips.
Discarding bay leaf and allspice, force the vegetables through food mill into the bowl containing
cooking liquid (or purée vegetables in an electric
blender). Pour into Dutch oven. Heat stew thoroughly.

6 to 8 servings

Oven Lamb Stew

    2 pounds boneless lean lamb shoulder, cut
       in 2-inch cubes
    1¾ teaspoons salt
    ¼ teaspoon thyme, crushed
    1 bay leaf
    4 whole allspice
    2 tablespoons chopped parsley
    1 clove garlic, minced
    ¼ small head cabbage, shredded
    2 leeks, thinly sliced
    2 medium-sized onions, sliced
    1 cup sliced raw potatoes
    8 small whole onions
    4 carrots, cut in 2-inch pieces
    2 white turnips, quartered

1. Put the lamb into a Dutch oven. Add salt,
thyme, bay leaf, allspice, parsley, garlic, cabbage,
leeks, sliced onions, potatoes, and about 4 cups
water. Cover tightly and bring rapidly to boiling.
2. Set in a 350°F oven and bake about 1½ hours, or
until meat is tender.
3. About 30 minutes before baking time is ended,

Oxtail Stew, German Style

    3 oxtails (about 1 pound each), disjointed
    ½ cup all-purpose flour
    1 teaspoon salt
    ¼ teaspoon pepper
    3 tablespoons butter or margarine
    1½ cups chopped onions
    1 can (28 ounces) tomatoes, drained
       (reserve liquid)
    1½ cups hot water
    4 potatoes, washed and pared
    6 carrots, pared
    2 pounds fresh peas, shelled
    1 tablespoon paprika
    1 teaspoon salt
    ¼ teaspoon pepper
    ¼ cup cold water
    2 tablespoons flour

1. Coat oxtail pieces evenly with a mixture of ½
cup flour, 1 teaspoon salt, and ¼ teaspoon pepper.
2. Heat the butter in a 3-quart Dutch oven over

low heat. Add onions and cook until tender, stirring occasionally. Remove onions with a slotted spoon and set aside. Add meat and brown on all sides.

3. Return onions to Dutch oven; add reserved tomato liquid and the hot water; cover and simmer 2½ to 3 hours, or until meat is nearly tender.

4. Meanwhile, using a ball-shaped cutter, cut the potatoes and carrots into small balls; cut the tomatoes into pieces.

5. When meat is almost tender, add potatoes, carrots, peas, paprika, and remaining salt and pepper. Cover and simmer 20 minutes, or until vegetables are tender. Add tomatoes and cook 10 minutes longer, or until meat is tender. Remove meat and vegetables; keep hot.

6. Bring cooking liquid to boiling and stir in a mixture of the cold water and 2 tablespoons flour; cook and stir 1 to 2 minutes. Return meat and vegetables and heat thoroughly.

6 to 8 servings

Ragout of Beef Hunstman

1 pound dried red kidney beans, washed
2 teaspoons salt
2 pounds beef chuck, cubed
    Salt and pepper
2 tablespoons shortening
4 onions, sliced
1 teaspoon paprika
1 teaspoon chili powder
3 cups red wine
½ yellow turnip (rutabaga), cubed
4 medium-sized potatoes, pared and cubed
1 bunch carrots, pared and sliced
3 cups water
2 cups canned tomatoes with liquid
2 cups cooked julienne green beans
3 tablespoons flour
2 cups dairy sour cream, chilled, or sour cream substitute (page 26)

1. Bring 6 cups water to boiling in a Dutch oven. Add kidney beans and boil 2 minutes. Cover, remove from heat, and let stand 1 hour.

2. Add 2 teaspoons salt to beans in soaking liquid and simmer covered 2 hours, or until tender.

3. Meanwhile, season beef with salt and pepper. Brown on all sides in shortening in a saucepot.

4. Add onions and sprinkle with paprika and chili powder. Cook onions until lightly browned, stirring occasionally. Add wine, cover, and simmer 2 hours.

5. Add the raw vegetables and water. Simmer, covered, until tender, about 45 minutes.

6. Add tomatoes, kidney beans, and green beans. Heat thoroughly. Thicken gravy with the flour (mixed with cold water to form a smooth paste). Serve with sour cream sprinkled with **paprika**.

6 servings

Spiced Short Ribs with Cabbage

3 pounds lean beef short ribs
2 tablespoons shortening
1 tablespoon dry mustard
2 teaspoons salt
¼ teaspoon pepper
½ teaspoon crushed oregano
⅛ teaspoon crushed sage
1 bay leaf
½ cup sliced onion
¼ cup sliced celery
1 cup water
½ cup cider vinegar
½ head cabbage, cut in 4 wedges

1. Add short ribs to heated shortening in a heavy skillet having a tight-fitting cover; brown meat well on all sides. Pour off excess fat.

2. Add a mixture of dry mustard, salt, pepper, oregano, and sage, then bay leaf, onion, celery, and a mixture of water and vinegar. Cover and cook slowly about 1½ hours, or until meat is almost tender.

3. Add cabbage wedges, cover, and cook about 25 minutes, or until tender. Add more liquid if necessary during cooking.

4. Serve ribs on a heated platter and surround with wedges of cabbage.

4 servings

MEAT

The meat counter is the place to ring up savings, as meat averages around 30 percent of the food bill. A little time spent learning how to cook the lower-priced cuts will pay big dividends.

Cuts that classify as "less tender" are usually the bargain buys. The challenge to the cook is to make them "more tender." This is done by pounding to break the fiber; through long, slow cooking in moist heat; and with tenderizers. Stews, pot roasts, and Swiss steaks are good examples of meat made tender through cooking.

There are both less tender and tender cuts in all grades of meat. Get acquainted with the cooking methods that make them all equally appetizing.

MEAT GRADING AND INSPECTION

Those purple marks on the fat of meat are government meat symbols. All meat is inspected; some meat is graded.

The *grade* of meat (not always shown) is in the shape of a shield. For beef, veal, and lamb, the top three grades are Prime, Choice, and Good. Most Prime cuts go to the restaurant trade; meat in the store is generally Choice or Good. Lower grades of beef are Standard, Commercial, Cutter, and Canner. All of these are wholesome, but the quality of lower grades is better suited to commercial processing than to home cooking.

There are grades for pork, too, from high to low (U.S. No. 1 through No. 4), but they are not widely used.

Many packers and retailers have established their own grade names. Government grading is not required by law; it is a voluntary service.

Meat inspection, on the other hand, is required for all packers involved in interstate trade. The circular mark is your assurance that the meat or poultry has met the approval of a federal inspector. It has come from a healthy animal and was processed in a sanitary plant.

LEARN TO FIGURE SERVINGS PER POUND

Is a particular cut a good buy? The best way to tell is to divide the total number of servings it will furnish into the price. Bony cuts of meat give fewer servings to the pound; therefore a low price tag won't mean as much as it will on a boneless cut.

Here is a chart showing the approximate number of servings in various cuts of meat. Keep in mind the size of appetites in your family; if you have small children, food will go farther.

Of course, all of these can be extended to extra servings by adding pasta, rice, or bread crumbs, as in meat loaves and other combinations.

TWO SERVINGS PER POUND

BEEF
Chuck blade steak
Chuck arm steak
Chuck roast (blade)
Chuck roast (arm)

PORK
Picnic (bone in)
Ham steaks

POULTRY
Broiler-fryer chicken, ready-to-cook

THREE SERVINGS PER POUND

BEEF
Chuck roast (boneless)
Brisket
Round
Sirloin tip

PORK
Blade steaks
Ham (bone in)
Boston butt (bone in)
Ribs, farm or country style

POULTRY
Legs, thighs

FOUR SERVINGS PER POUND

BEEF
Ground beef

PORK
Center cut or rib chops
Sausage
Ham (boneless and canned)

POULTRY
Breasts

FISH
Fillets, steaks, sticks

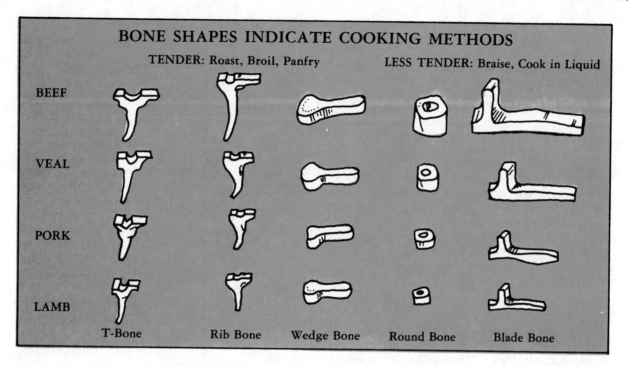

BONE SHAPES INDICATE COOKING METHODS

TENDER: Roast, Broil, Panfry   **LESS TENDER: Braise, Cook in Liquid**

BEEF · VEAL · PORK · LAMB

T-Bone   Rib Bone   Wedge Bone   Round Bone   Blade Bone

THE BONE SHAPE IS A GUIDE TO TENDERNESS

How can a shopper judge tender from less-tender meat? The bone shape is one clue. The presence of a blade bone in meat nearly always indicates less-tender meat. In beef, a round bone does, too. But if you find a rib, wedge, or T-bone you know you can use a quick-cooking method.

Pot Roast Piquante

3- to 4-pound beef pot roast
¼ cup flour
2 teaspoons salt
¼ teaspoon black pepper
2 tablespoons cooking oil
1 can (16 ounces) tomatoes
2 onions, halved and sliced
½ cup sliced pitted ripe olives
½ teaspoon chili powder
1 ripe avocado, sliced (optional)

1. Coat meat with a mixture of flour, salt, and pepper.
2. Brown meat on both sides in hot oil in a large, heavy skillet.
3. Mix in the tomatoes, onions, olives, and chili powder. Cover and simmer until meat is tender, about 3 hours.
4. Remove meat to warm serving platter and pour gravy over meat. Arrange avocado slices (drizzled with **lemon juice** to prevent discoloration) on top of pot roast and garnish with thin **lemon cartwheels**.

About 8 servings

Porcupine Beef Balls in Tomato Sauce

1 pound ground beef
½ cup uncooked rice
¼ cup minced onion
1 teaspoon salt
⅛ teaspoon pepper
1½ cups tomato juice or 1 can (about 10 ounces) condensed tomato soup plus ½ cup water
1 teaspoon Worcestershire sauce

1. Mix together ground beef, rice, onion, salt, and pepper. Form into 8 balls, and place in greased baking dish having a tight-fitting cover.
2. In a saucepan, combine the tomato juice and Worcestershire sauce. Heat to boiling and pour over meatballs.
3. Cover and bake at 350°F about 1¼ hours, or until visible rice is tender when pressed lightly between fingers. Serve with tomato sauce.

4 to 6 servings

Versatile Meat-Vegetable Casserole

2 large onions, chopped (about 2 cups)
2 tablespoons margarine
1 can (10½ ounces) chicken gravy
2 cups diced cooked meat (beef, lamb, chicken, or turkey)
    Salt and pepper to taste
2 cups cooked vegetables (any kind)
2 cups mashed potatoes
¼ cup Seasoned Crumbs

1. Brown onion in skillet in 1 tablespoon margarine. Stir in gravy and meat; season with salt and pepper. Spread in a greased 2-quart casserole.
2. Top with vegetables, then potatoes.
3. Dot with remaining 1 tablespoon margarine and sprinkle with Seasoned Crumbs.
4. Bake at 425°F 20 to 25 minutes, or until top is brown and gravy bubbles.

6 to 8 servings

Seasoned Crumbs: Sauté 1 tablespoon onion in 2 tablespoons margarine. Add ½ cup fine dry bread crumbs and cook, stirring constantly, until crumbs are browned.

Meat Loaf à la Wellington

¾ pound medium mushrooms
1½ pounds ground lean beef
¾ cup soft bread crumbs
½ cup minced onion
⅓ cup ketchup
2 eggs, slightly beaten
2 teaspoons salt
¼ teaspoon black pepper
⅓ pound liver sausage
2 sticks pie crust mix
    Beaten egg for brushing

1. Rinse, dry, and trim stems of mushrooms. Reserve 6 whole mushrooms. Finely chop remaining mushrooms; put into a large bowl. Add beef, bread crumbs, onion, ketchup, eggs, salt, and pepper; mix lightly.
2. Shape half of the meat mixture into a 9×4-inch rectangle on a jelly-roll or shallow baking pan.

Make a slight indentation lengthwise in center of meat rectangle. Place reserved mushrooms in well, stem ends down. Cover with remaining meat mixture; pat gently into shape, rounding top.
3. Bake at 350°F about 1 hour, or until done as desired.
4. Remove meat loaf from oven and set aside to cool.
5. Beat liver sausage with a fork and spread over top of meat loaf.
6. Prepare pie crust mix, following package directions. Roll out on a lightly floured pastry canvas into a rectangle about 18×12 inches. Center pastry over top of meat loaf; overlap bottom about ½ inch. Seal. Bring sides of pastry to bottom; overlap and seal, trimming ends if necessary. Place on a baking sheet. Brush top and sides with beaten egg. Use remaining scraps of pastry for making decoration for top; press firmly in place.
7. Bake at 400°F about 30 minutes, or until lightly browned. Let stand about 10 minutes before carving.

About 6 servings

Ground Beef-Eggplant Casserole

1 large or 2 small eggplants, pared and cut in ½-inch slices
    Vegetable oil
1½ pounds lean ground beef
¾ teaspoon salt
½ teaspoon monosodium glutamate
⅛ teaspoon black pepper
¼ cup chopped onion
1 clove garlic, minced
½ cup chopped green pepper
2 cans beef gravy-sauce with tomato
¾ teaspoon crushed basil
¼ pound thinly sliced mozzarella cheese
¼ cup fine dry bread crumbs
1 tablespoon butter or margarine

1. Brown eggplant slices in a small amount of hot oil in a large skillet. Remove from skillet and set aside.
2. Mix the ground beef with salt, monosodium glutamate, and pepper; set aside.
3. Add about 2 tablespoons oil to the skillet. Add onion, garlic, and green pepper to hot oil and cook about 2 minutes, stirring occasionally. Add the meat and cook until it has lost its pink color, stirring occasionally.

4. Remove from heat and stir in a mixture of the gravy-sauce and basil.

5. Spoon about one third of the meat sauce over the bottom of a 2-quart baking dish. Arrange half the eggplant slices in a layer over the sauce. Place slices of cheese over the eggplant. Repeat with meat sauce and eggplant; end with remaining meat sauce. Sprinkle a mixture of the bread crumbs and butter over the top.

6. Set in a 375°F oven about 20 minutes, or until mixture is thoroughly heated and topping is browned. Accompany with **buttered noodles** and a **crisp green salad.**

About 8 servings

Beef Sirloin Tip Roast with Parmesan Barbecue Baste

   1 **sirloin tip roast (3½ to 5 pounds)**
      Parmesan Barbecue Baste

1. Place roast, fat side up, in a shallow roasting pan. Insert meat thermometer so bulb is centered in the thickest part. Do not add water. Do not cover.

2. Roast at 325°F. Roast is done when meat thermometer registers 140°F for rare; 160°F for medium; and 170°F for well done. Brush with Parmesan Barbecue Baste occasionally during the last 30 minutes cooking time.

3. For a 3½- to 5-pound roast, allow 35 to 40 minutes per pound. For a 6- to 8-pound roast, allow 30 to 35 minutes per pound.

4. For easier carving, allow roast to "stand" in a warm place 15 to 20 minutes after removal from oven. Since roast usually continues to cook after removal from oven, it is best to remove it about 5°F below the temperature desired.

Parmesan Barbecue Baste

   ¾ **cup ketchup**
   ½ **cup chopped onion**
   ¼ **cup water**
   2 **tablespoons Parmesan cheese**
   1 **tablespoon Worcestershire sauce**

Combine ketchup, onion, water, Parmesan cheese, and Worcestershire sauce in small saucepan. Cook slowly, for 5 to 10 minutes, stirring occasionally.

Swiss Steak in Vegetable Sauce

   ¼ **cup flour**
   ½ **teaspoon monosodium glutamate**
   ¼ **teaspoon salt**
      Few grains pepper
 1½ **pounds beef round, blade, or arm steak, cut 1¼ inches thick**
   2 **tablespoons butter or margarine**
   1 **can (about 10 ounces) condensed beef broth**
   ½ **to ¾ cup hot water**
   ½ **bay leaf**
  ⅛ **teaspoon ground cinnamon**
   1 **can (about 10 ounces) condensed vegetable soup**
  ⅓ **cup ketchup**

1. Mix the flour, monosodium glutamate, salt, and pepper and pound into the meat with a meat hammer, using one half of mixture for each side.

2. Heat butter in a Dutch oven or heavy saucepot; add steak and brown evenly on both sides.

3. Add broth, hot water, bay leaf, and cinnamon. Cover pot and bring liquid rapidly to boiling; reduce heat and simmer until steak is tender, 60 to 75 minutes.

4. Remove meat to a platter and keep warm.

5. Pour the vegetable soup and ketchup into the pot; heat thoroughly, stirring to blend in brown residue on bottom. Remove bay leaf; pour sauce over meat and serve immediately.

About 6 servings

Savory Swiss Steak Strips

½ cup flour
½ teaspoon salt
½ teaspoon paprika
  Dash pepper
3 pounds beef round steak, cut in ¾-inch strips
¼ cup vegetable oil
1 cup thinly sliced onions
1 clove garlic, crushed
3 cups beef bouillon
½ teaspoon salt
½ teaspoon leaf thyme
1 bay leaf

1. Combine flour, salt, paprika, and pepper. Coat meat with mixture. Reserve 3 tablespoons of seasoned flour mixture. Brown meat in hot oil; remove from pan to a baking dish.
2. Sauté onion and garlic in remaining oil for about 3 minutes. Mix in reserved seasoned flour.
3. Add bouillon, salt, thyme, and bay leaf; mix well. Pour bouillon mixture over meat; cover.
4. Bake at 325°F 1½ hours, or until beef is tender. Serve over **rice** or **noodles**.

8 servings

Patchwork Casserole

2 pounds ground beef
2 cups chopped green pepper
1 cup chopped onion
2 pounds frozen southern-style hash brown potatoes
2 cans (8 ounces each) tomato sauce
1 can (6 ounces) tomato paste
1 cup water
1 teaspoon salt
½ teaspoon basil
¼ teaspoon pepper
1 pound pasteurized process American cheese, thinly sliced

1. Brown the meat in a large skillet just until meat is no longer pink. Drain off excess fat. Add green pepper and onion; cook until tender, stirring occasionally. Add remaining ingredients except cheese; mix well.
2. Spoon half of meat-and-potato mixture into a 3-quart baking dish (13½×8¾-inch) or two 1½-quart casseroles. Cover with half of cheese. Spoon remaining meat-and-potato mixture into dish. Cover dish tightly with aluminum foil.
3. Bake at 350°F 45 minutes.
4. Cut remaining cheese into decorative shapes.
5. Remove foil from dish and arrange cheese in a patchwork design. Let stand about 5 minutes, or until cheese is softened.

12 to 16 servings

Roast Pork, Pennsylvania Dutch Style

1 pork loin roast (6 pounds)
¼ cup flour
1¼ teaspoons salt
1 teaspoon ground ginger
¼ teaspoon pepper
1 cup hot water
2 onions, thinly sliced
2 tablespoons flour
1½ cups water

1. Have meat dealer loosen chine bone. Rub meat with a mixture of the flour, salt, ginger, and pepper. Place roast, fat side up, in a shallow pan. Insert meat thermometer so tip is slightly beyond center of largest muscle, being sure the tip does not rest in fat or on bone.
2. Roast, uncovered, at 400°F 45 minutes. Turn oven temperature to 350°F and continue roasting about 1¾ hours. After the first hour, add the hot water and sliced onions; baste every 15 minutes. Meat is done when internal temperature reaches 170°F.

3. Place roast on a hot serving platter; remove thermometer and keep roast hot.

4. Stir the remaining flour into drippings in pan. Stirring constantly, add the 1½ cups water, bring rapidly to boiling, and cook 1 to 2 minutes. Serve with the roast.

8 to 12 servings

Green Bean-Pork Chop Casserole

2 teaspoons fat
6 pork chops, cut ½ to ¾ inch thick
2 cans (16 ounces each) cut green beans, drained (reserve 2 tablespoons liquid)
1 can (12 ounces) whole kernel corn
1 tablespoon cornstarch
1 can (8 ounces) tomato sauce
1 tablespoon finely chopped onion
1 tablespoon salt
¼ teaspoon black pepper
¼ teaspoon chervil, crushed
1 teaspoon Worcestershire sauce

1. Heat fat in a large, heavy skillet. Add chops and brown on all sides.

2. Mix beans and corn in a 2½-quart casserole.

3. Blend the reserved bean liquid with cornstarch; stir in the remaining ingredients. Pour sauce over vegetables and toss until well coated. Arrange chops on top of vegetable mixture.

4. Bake, covered, at 350°F 1 hour, or until pork chops are tender. Uncover and bake 10 minutes longer.

6 servings

Spicy Lamb Superb

¼ teaspoon ground ginger
¼ teaspoon ground allspice
¼ teaspoon ground cinnamon
¼ teaspoon oregano
⅛ teaspoon curry powder
1 bay leaf
1 can (8 ounces) tomato sauce
¾ cup unsweetened pineapple juice
6 lamb shoulder chops, cut ½ inch thick

1. Mix the ginger, allspice, cinnamon, oregano, curry powder, and bay leaf in a saucepan. Blend in the tomato sauce and pineapple juice. Bring mix-

ture to boiling; simmer, uncovered, 5 minutes. Cool; remove bay leaf.

2. Arrange chops in a large, shallow dish. Pour sauce over chops. Refrigerate about 8 hours.

3. Broil chops 3 inches from source of heat about 15 minutes on each side, brushing with marinade.

6 servings

Smoked Shoulder Roll with Mustard Sauce

Cooked smoked shoulder roll (see recipe)
⅓ cup packed brown sugar
2 teaspoons flour
1 teaspoon prepared mustard
½ cup water
3 tablespoons cider vinegar
2 egg yolks, slightly beaten
1 tablespoon butter or margarine
1 package (10 ounces) frozen broccoli spears
1 package (10 ounces) frozen cauliflower
½ cup shredded sharp Cheddar cheese (about 2 ounces)

1. Slice cooked shoulder roll.

2. Combine brown sugar and flour in top of double boiler. Stir in mustard, then water and vinegar. Continue stirring and bring to boiling over direct heat; cook 3 minutes.

3. Remove from heat and vigorously stir about 3 tablespoons of hot mixture into beaten egg yolks; immediately blend into mixture in double boiler.

4. Cook over hot water 3 to 5 minutes; stir slowly. Remove from heat and stir in the butter.

5. Cook broccoli and cauliflower according to directions on package; drain, if necessary.

6. Arrange shoulder butt slices in a shallow baking dish. Arrange broccoli spears and cauliflower over meat. Spoon mustard sauce over all and top evenly with cheese.

7. Set in a 350°F oven about 15 minutes, or until thoroughly heated.

4 servings

Cooked Smoked Shoulder Roll: Put a 1½-pound smoked pork shoulder roll (butt) into a large heavy saucepot. Add enough hot water to cover meat. Add 1 teaspoon monosodium glutamate, 5 whole cloves, 3 peppercorns, and 1 clove garlic. Bring liquid to boiling; reduce heat, cover and simmer (do not boil) about 1 hour, or until meat is tender.

Barbecued Lamb Shanks

    4 lamb shanks, about 1 pound each
    ¼ cup flour
    1 teaspoon salt
    ¼ teaspoon pepper
    ¼ cup fat
    1 cup chopped onion
    2 cloves garlic, minced
    1 cup ketchup
    ½ cup water
    ¼ cup wine vinegar
    4 teaspoons Worcestershire sauce
    5 drops Tabasco
    2 teaspoons sugar
    2 teaspoons paprika
    1 teaspoon dry mustard
    1 teaspoon salt
    ½ teaspoon pepper

1. Coat the lamb shanks evenly with a mixture of the flour, 1 teaspoon salt, and ¼ teaspoon pepper.
2. Heat fat in a large, heavy skillet over medium heat. Add shanks and brown well on all sides. Remove meat to a large, shallow baking dish.
3. Meanwhile, combine the onion, garlic, ketchup, water, vinegar, Worcestershire sauce, and Tabasco in a saucepan. Stir in a mixture of sugar, paprika, dry mustard, salt, and pepper and heat to boiling. Pour sauce over lamb.
4. Bake, covered, at 300°F 1½ to 2 hours, or until meat is tender; turn shanks and baste frequently with the sauce.

About 4 servings

Herbed Lamb Kidneys in Rice Ring

    ¾ cup butter or margarine
    1 clove garlic, crushed
    ½ pound fresh mushrooms, sliced
         lengthwise
    1 large onion, sliced
    ¼ teaspoon salt
    ⅛ teaspoon pepper
    3 to 4 tablespoons lemon juice
    1 tablespoon crushed rosemary
   12 lamb kidneys, cut in half lengthwise
         and trimmed
         Parsley Rice Ring

1. Heat butter in a large skillet. Add garlic, mushrooms, onion, salt, and pepper; cook until mushrooms and onion are lightly browned, stirring occasionally. Remove vegetables; keep warm.
2. Mix lemon juice and rosemary into butter remaining in skillet. Add kidneys and cook about 10 minutes, or until kidneys are tender but still slightly pink in center; turn frequently.
3. Return vegetables to the skillet and mix lightly with the kidneys. Spoon into center of rice ring. Serve remaining sauce in a gravy boat.

6 to 8 servings

Parsley Rice Ring: Bring 4 cups **chicken broth** to boiling; add **2 cups uncooked rice** and 2 **teaspoons salt**. Cover and cook over low heat for time indicated on rice package, or until rice is tender and liquid is absorbed. Stir ¼ **cup butter** and ½ **cup snipped parsley** into the cooked rice until well blended. Pack into a lightly buttered 5½-cup ring mold. Let stand 10 minutes; unmold onto a warm serving plate.

Liver à la Madame Begue

    1 pound liver, cut in 1-inch cubes
    1 teaspoon salt
       Few grains pepper
    2 small onions, thinly sliced
    3 large sprigs parsley
       Fat for deep frying heated to 390°F

1. Sprinkle liver with salt and pepper. Put into a bowl; cover with onion and parsley. Cover and refrigerate 2 hours.
2. Fry liver, onion, and parsley in the heated fat 40

to 60 seconds or until just done. Drain over fat for a few seconds before removing. Serve immediately, garnished with lemon wedges and parsley, if desired.

4 servings

Liver on Skewers

    1 **pound liver**
    Salt, pepper, and ground sage
    Bacon slices

1. Cut liver into chunks. Season with salt, pepper, and sage.
2. Thread liver and bacon onto 4 skewers, keeping bacon slice in one piece and placing a liver chunk in each loop of bacon.
3. Grill in broiler or over an open fire until done.

4 servings

Glazed Stuffed Beef Heart

    1 **beef heart (3 to 3½ pounds)**
    ¼ **cup butter or margarine**
    ¼ **cup finely chopped onion**
    1 **quart soft bread crumbs**
    1 **tablespoon minced parsley**
    1 **teaspoon poultry seasoning**
    ¼ **teaspoon salt**
    Few grains pepper
    3 **tablespoons fat**
    1 **cup finely chopped onion**
    3 **cups hot water**
    3 **cups beef broth**
    2 **teaspoons salt**
    ¼ **teaspoon pepper**
    1 **teaspoon celery salt**
    1 **teaspoon marjoram**
    ½ **cup red currant jelly**
    1 **tablespoon water**
    Gravy

1. Cut arteries, veins, and any hard parts from beef heart, making pocket for stuffing. Wash and set aside to drain.
2. Heat ¼ cup butter in a skillet; add ¼ cup chopped onion and cook until soft.
3. Turn contents of skillet into a large bowl containing a mixture of the bread crumbs, parsley, poultry seasoning, ¼ teaspoon salt, and few grains pepper; mix lightly. Stuff heart with the mixture and fasten with skewers; set aside.
4. Heat fat in a Dutch oven. Add 1 cup onion and cook until onion is soft; remove onion and set aside.

5. Put beef heart into the Dutch oven; brown lightly on all sides. Add water, beef broth, salt, pepper, celery salt, and cooked onion to Dutch oven. Bring liquid rapidly to boiling; reduce heat, cover and simmer 2½ to 3 hours, or until heart is tender. Mix in marjoram 15 minutes before end of cooking.
6. Heat jelly and water together over very low heat until jelly is melted, stirring occasionally.
7. Remove heart from liquid. Strain and reserve cooking liquid for gravy.
8. Brush beef heart with the jelly to glaze; serve with gravy.

About 8 servings

Gravy: Measure 3 cups of the reserved cooking liquid. Heat ⅓ **cup butter or margarine** in the Dutch oven. Blend in ⅓ **cup flour.** Heat until mixture bubbles and flour is lightly browned. Remove from heat and stir in the reserved cooking liquid and 2 **teaspoons lemon juice.** Return to heat. Bring rapidly to boiling, stirring constantly, and cook until mixture thickens; cook 1 to 2 minutes longer.

Sweetbreads aux Capres

    5 **pounds sweetbreads, rinsed in cold**
      water
    2 **cups dry white wine**
    1 **to 2 tablespoons mixed pickling spices**
    1 **medium-sized onion, quartered**
    2 **stalks celery**
    1 **tablespoon salt**
    Butter
    1 **heaping teaspoon capers**
    Lemon juice

1. Put sweetbreads into a heavy casserole. Cover with water. Add wine, pickling spices, onion, celery, and salt. Poach gently until done, about 1½ hours. Chill.
2. Separate sweetbreads into bite-sized pieces, dust with **flour, salt,** and **pepper,** and sauté in butter until golden brown and a little crisp. Remove from pan to a warm plate.
3. Add capers and a few drops lemon juice to butter in pan. Pour sauce over sweetbreads. Garnish with **watercress.**

10 to 15 servings

Note: The strained broth makes excellent stock for lima bean, mushroom, or barley soup.

FISH

If you're blessed with a lot of free time and a good fishing pole, you can bring home your own bargains. Most of us must find them at the store.

Watch for specials on both the fresh-water fish and seafood. Fish is an excellent buy for calorie-watchers, as well as money-watchers, so it pays to learn how to cook it in a number of ways. Don't fall into the old flour-it-and-fry-it rut; learn to poach, bake, and charcoal grill as well.

Canned fish offers many possibilities, too. You are already familiar with tuna and probably use it in few specialities of your own. You've found that it's interchangeable with salmon when that popular fish is on special. If you've experimented with mackerel, with its lowest-of-all price tag, you've found that it can go just about anywhere that tuna and salmon are used.

Fish sticks from the freezer case are generally budget priced and easy to fix. Just keep in mind that they are not all fish; a portion of the weight is breading.

Fish Fillets

    2 pounds fresh or frozen fish fillets,
        thawed
    ½ cup yellow cornmeal
    1½ teaspoons salt
    ⅛ teaspoon pepper
        Shortening

1. Cut the fillets into serving-sized pieces. Coat with a mixture of cornmeal, salt, and pepper.
2. Fry in hot shortening in a skillet until crisp and browned on both sides.

About 6 servings

Fried Smelts

    2 dozen smelts
    1 egg, beaten
    1 tablespoon water
        Fine bread crumbs
        Fat for deep frying heated to 360°F

1. Clean smelts by drawing a sharp knife over the skin to remove scales. Remove head and tail. Make a slit in underside and pull out entrails.
2. Sprinkle with **salt** and **pepper**; shake in a bag with **flour**; dip in a mixture of the egg and water; roll in crumbs. Let stand about 15 minutes.
3. Fry smelts without crowding in heated fat 3 to 4 minutes. Drain on absorbent paper.
4. Garnish with **parsley**; serve with **tartar sauce**.

4 servings

Planked Fish Fillet Dinner

    1 large fish fillet, weighing about 10
        ounces (such as sole, flounder,
        whitefish, lake trout, or haddock)
    1 tablespoon melted butter or margarine
        Salt and pepper
        Seasoned instant potatoes
    2 broiled tomato halves
    4 broiled mushroom caps (optional)
        Lemon slices
        Watercress or parsley

1. If fish is frozen, let thaw on refrigerator shelf or at room temperature. Brush seasoned plank lightly with melted butter.
2. Place fish fillet on plank and brush with remaining butter. Sprinkle lightly with salt and pepper. Bake at 350°F for 20 minutes, or just until fish flakes easily.
3. Remove from oven, and turn oven temperature up to 450°F. Pipe a border of hot mashed potatoes along sides of fish.
4. Return to oven for 10 minutes until potatoes are delicately browned. Place tomato halves and mushroom caps, if desired, on plank. Garnish with lemon slices and watercress. Serve at once.

2 servings

Fish Poached in Court Bouillon

    1 quart water
    ½ cup vinegar
    1 carrot, sliced
    2 small onions, sliced
    3 or 4 shallots, minced
    ½ lemon, sliced
    1 teaspoon salt
        Herb bouquet
    4 peppercorns
    1 fish (about 2 pounds)

1. Heat the water in a large kettle with vinegar, carrot, onions, shallots, lemon, salt, and herb bou-

quet. Bring to boiling; reduce heat, cover, and simmer 20 minutes.
2. Add peppercorns and cook 10 minutes longer; strain and set aside.
3. Place fish in a large skillet. Cover with hot court bouillon and poach, covered, over low heat. Allow about 8 minutes per pound, or until fish flakes easily. Drain.
4. Serve hot with **melted butter**.

About 4 servings

Herb bouquet: Enclose herbs (such as a piece of **celery with leaves**, a sprig of **thyme**, 3 or 4 sprigs of **parsley**, and a **bay leaf**) in a cheesecloth bag.

Skillet Tuna Supreme

⅔ cup chopped onion
1 green pepper, cut in slivers
2 tablespoons vegetable oil
1 can (about 10 ounces) condensed tomato soup
2 teaspoons soy sauce
2 to 3 tablespoons brown sugar
1 teaspoon grated lemon peel
3 tablespoons lemon juice
2 cans (6½ or 7 ounces each) tuna, drained

1. Cook onion and green pepper until almost tender in hot oil in a large skillet; stir occasionally.
2. Mix in the tomato soup, soy sauce, brown sugar,

and lemon peel and juice. Bring to boiling; simmer 5 minutes.
3. Mix in the tuna, separating it into small pieces. Heat thoroughly.
4. Serve with **fluffy hot cooked rice** or **chow mein noodles**.

About 6 servings

Tuna-Chili Chowder

3 cans (6½ or 7 ounces each) tuna packed in oil, drained and separated in large pieces (reserve ¼ cup oil)
1 cup sliced celery
1 cup chopped green pepper
3 onions, chopped
1½ teaspoons paprika
1 can (about 10 ounces) condensed tomato soup
3 soup cans water
2 tablespoons tomato paste
2 tablespoons cider vinegar
1 teaspoon salt
¼ teaspoon pepper
1½ teaspoons chili powder
2 cans (about 16 ounces each) red kidney beans, drained

1. Heat the tuna oil in a large saucepan. Add the celery, green pepper, onion, and paprika; cook over medium heat, stirring occasionally, until celery is just tender.
2. Mix in remaining ingredients and the tuna. Cover and simmer to blend flavors.

About 8 servings

Tuna Casserole

1 can (6½ or 7 ounces) tuna packed in oil
1 pound creamed cottage cheese
¾ teaspoon salt
¼ teaspoon white pepper
¾ cup fine dry bread crumbs
4 eggs, beaten
1 tablespoon butter or margarine, melted

1. Empty tuna with its oil into a bowl. Separate tuna into chunks. Add cottage cheese, salt, pepper, ½ cup bread crumbs, and beaten eggs; mix well. Turn into a greased 1½-quart casserole.
2. Mix remaining ¼ cup bread crumbs with melted butter. Sprinkle over casserole mixture.
3. Bake at 350°F about 30 minutes, or until set.

About 6 servings

Choose-a-Partner Tuna Casserole

2 cans (6½ or 7 ounces each) tuna in vegetable oil
1 teaspoon salt
  Pasta or rice ingredient, cooked following package directions
  Frozen vegetable, thawed
  Sauce
  Extra ingredients (optional)

1. In a large bowl mix tuna, salt, cooked pasta or rice, thawed frozen vegetable, and sauce. Add one or more extra ingredients, if desired.
2. Turn into a greased 2-quart casserole; cover.
3. Bake at 350°F 50 to 60 minutes.

6 servings

CHOOSE A PASTA OR RICE INGREDIENT:

2 cups uncooked elbow macaroni
1 cup uncooked regular rice
4 cups uncooked broad egg noodles
4 cups uncooked large macaroni shells
3 cups uncooked medium macaroni shells
4 cups uncooked bow ties

CHOOSE A FROZEN VEGETABLE:

1 package (10 ounces) frozen chopped spinach
1 package (10 ounces) frozen chopped broccoli
1 package (9 ounces) frozen Italian green beans
1 package (10 ounces) frozen green peas
1 package (10 ounces) frozen mixed vegetables

CHOOSE A SAUCE:

1 can (about 10 ounces) condensed cream of mushroom soup plus 1 cup milk
1 can (about 10 ounces) condensed cream of celery soup plus 1¼ cups milk
1 can (about 10 ounces) condensed cream of chicken soup plus 1¼ cups milk
1 can (about 10 ounces) condensed cream of asparagus soup plus 1¼ cups milk
1 can (about 10 ounces) condensed Cheddar cheese soup plus 1¼ cups milk
1 can (16 ounces) seasoned stewed tomatoes

CHOOSE ONE OR MORE EXTRAS, IF DESIRED:

2 tablespoons grated Parmesan cheese
¼ cup shredded Swiss cheese
1 can (3 ounces) sliced mushrooms, drained
¼ cup sliced ripe olives
¼ cup chopped green pepper
¼ cup chopped onion
¼ cup chopped celery

SAMPLE CASSEROLE COMBINATIONS

Tuna and Noodle Casserole Florentine: Use broad noodles, chopped spinach, mushroom soup, and Swiss cheese.

Tuna, Broccoli, and Macaroni Casserole: Use elbow macaroni, chopped broccoli, cheese soup, and chopped celery.

Tuna, Green Beans, and Rice Casserole: Use rice, Italian green beans, stewed tomatoes, and Parmesan cheese.

Fish Stick Special

1 package (10 ounces) frozen fish sticks
1 cup shredded Cheddar cheese (about 4 ounces)
½ cup chopped sweet mixed pickles
¼ cup milk
2 tablespoons chopped onion
¼ cup buttered dry bread crumbs

1. Arrange fish sticks in a shallow baking dish.
2. Mix the remaining ingredients except bread crumbs and spoon over fish. Top with crumbs.
3. Heat in a 425°F oven 15 to 20 minutes.

About 4 servings

Blushing Tuna Pie

3 cans (6½ or 7 ounces each) chunk-style tuna packed in oil, drained (reserve 3 tablespoons oil)
⅔ cup ketchup
½ teaspoon salt
2 tablespoons flour
¼ teaspoon pepper
1½ cups milk
1 cup shredded sharp Cheddar cheese (about 4 ounces)
½ teaspoon Worcestershire sauce
1 unbaked 9-inch pastry shell (see page 19)

1. Mix tuna, ketchup, and salt in a bowl.
2. Put reserved tuna oil into a saucepan. Blend in flour and pepper. Heat until bubbly. Gradually add the milk, stirring constantly. Bring to boiling; cook 1 to 2 minutes.
3. Remove from heat. Add the cheese and stir until melted. Add the Worcestershire sauce and tuna; mix well. Turn into the unbaked pastry shell. Sprinkle with **paprika**.
4. Bake at 400°F 30 to 35 minutes, or until pastry is golden brown and mixture is bubbly.
5. Remove from oven and sprinkle lightly with snipped parsley.

4 servings

Mackerel Casserole

¼ cup butter or margarine
1 tablespoon minced onion
1 tablespoon chopped green pepper
¼ cup flour
1 teaspoon salt
½ teaspoon paprika
2 cups milk
2 cans (7 ounces each) or 1 can (about 16 ounces) mackerel, drained and rinsed
½ cup fine dry bread crumbs
2 tablespoons butter or margarine, melted

1. Heat butter in a skillet, add onion and green pepper, and sauté 2 minutes. Stir in flour, salt, and paprika. Add milk gradually, stirring constantly. Bring to boiling; cook and stir until thickened. Mix in mackerel.
2. Mix bread crumbs with melted butter. Alternate layers of sauce and crumbs in a greased 1-quart casserole; end with crumbs. Cover casserole.
3. Heat in a 375°F oven 30 minutes.

4 or 5 servings

Mackerel Patties

1 can (15 ounces) mackerel, drained and flaked
1½ cups soft bread crumbs
½ cup minced celery
3 tablespoons minced onion
3 tablespoons minced parsley
1 egg
½ teaspoon prepared horseradish
¼ teaspoon salt
Dash of pepper
3 tablespoons butter or shortening
Lemon wedges or ketchup

1. Mix mackerel, bread crumbs, celery, onion, parsley, egg, horseradish, salt, and pepper in bowl.
2. Shape into 4 or 5 patties. Heat butter in large skillet over medium heat.
3. Fry patties 3 or 4 minutes on each side, or until well browned. Serve with lemon wedges.

4 or 5 servings

Mackerel and Macaroni with Green Beans

2 cans (7 ounces each) or 1 can (about 16 ounces) mackerel
8 ounces elbow macaroni
2 cans (about 10 ounces each) condensed cream of mushroom soup
1¼ cups milk
1½ cups cubed sharp Cheddar cheese
1 tablespoon Worcestershire sauce
½ teaspoon savory
1 can (16 ounces) cut green beans, drained
½ cup buttered bread crumbs

1. Drain and rinse mackerel; set aside.
2. Cook the macaroni following package directions; drain.
3. Combine soup, milk, and cheese in a saucepan and heat until cheese is melted. Remove from heat; add Worcestershire sauce, savory, mackerel, and beans; mix well.
4. Put half the cooked macaroni into a greased 2½-quart casserole. Pour half the mackerel-cheese sauce over macaroni. Repeat layers. Sprinkle top with bread crumbs.
5. Bake at 325°F 30 minutes, or until crumbs are lightly browned.

6 to 8 servings

POULTRY

Look into the recipe file of any serious budgeter, and you're sure to come across a whole section on poultry. Chicken and turkey have more going for you than low prices; they offer welcome diversion from hamburger and tuna.

When buying chicken, you'll find the lowest price tags on whole birds. This tends to put off many buyers who have never tried to do the cutting themselves. It's a skill well worth learning, and not too difficult. A sharp knife, a cutting board, and the instructions on page 60 are all you need.

Save the giblets in an airtight bag in the freezer until you've collected enough to simmer for stock. Use it as the cooking liquid for rice, or in soups and gravies. The giblets are tasty additions to omelets and crêpes, or you can chop the livers for pâté.

Turkey is another good budget buy, especially when it's the week's special at the supermarket. One good-sized turkey can provide three or four main dishes, hearty sandwiches for the lunchbox, and a savory soup at the end of the week.

Like fish, poultry is lower in calories than most red meats, a factor that's as important as cost savings to many shoppers.

Roast Turkey with Cooked Giblets

1 ready-to-cook turkey (12 to 20 pounds)
Cooked Giblets and Broth (see recipe)
Herbed Stuffing (see recipe)
Salt
Melted fat
Turkey Roasting Pan Gravy (see recipe)

1. Rinse bird with cold water. Drain and pat dry with absorbent paper or soft cloth.
2. Prepare Cooked Giblets and Broth for gravy.
3. Prepare Herbed Stuffing.
4. Rub body and neck cavities with salt. Fill lightly with stuffing. (Extra stuffing may be put into a greased covered baking dish or wrapped in aluminum foil and baked with turkey the last hour of roasting time.)
5. Fasten neck skin to back with skewer and bring wing tips onto back. Push drumsticks under band of skin at tail, or tie with cord. Set, breast up, on rack in shallow roasting pan. Brush with melted fat.

6. If meat thermometer is used, place it in center of inside thigh muscle or thickest part of breast meat. Be sure that tip does not touch bone. If desired, cover top and sides of turkey with cheesecloth moistened with melted fat. Keep cloth moist during roasting by brushing occasionally with fat from the bottom of pan.
7. Roast, uncovered, at 325°F until turkey tests done (the thickest part of the drumstick feels soft when pressed with fingers and meat thermometer registers 180° to 185°F). See Timetable for Roasting Turkey. When turkey is two thirds done, cut band of skin or cord at drumsticks.
8. For easier carving, let turkey stand 20 to 30 minutes, keeping it warm. Meanwhile, prepare Turkey Roasting Pan Gravy from drippings.
9. Remove cord and skewers from turkey and place turkey on heated platter. Garnish platter, if desired.

TIMETABLE FOR ROASTING TURKEY AT 325°F

(For turkey thawed sufficiently to remove giblets, stuffed, then cooked to 180° to 185°F).

Ready-to-cook Weight (pounds)	Approximate Time (Hours) Uncovered Pan	Covered Pan
6 to 8	3 to 3½	2½ to 3
8 to 12	3½ to 4½	3 to 3½
12 to 16	4½ to 5½	3½ to 4
16 to 20	5½ to 6½	4 to 4½
20 to 24	6½ to 7¼	4½ to 5

Cooked Giblets and Broth: Put **turkey neck** and **giblets** (except liver) into a saucepan with **1 large onion,** sliced, **parsley, celery with leaves, 1 medium-sized bay leaf, 2 teaspoons salt,** and **1 quart water.** Cover and simmer until giblets are tender, about 2 hours; add the **liver** the last 15 minutes of cooking. Strain; reserve broth for gravy. Chop the giblets; set aside for gravy.

Herbed Stuffing

Cooked Giblets and Broth (see recipe)
4 quarts ½-inch bread cubes
1 cup snipped parsley
2 to 2½ teaspoons salt
2 teaspoons thyme
2 teaspoons rosemary, crushed
2 teaspoons marjoram
1 teaspoon ground sage
1 cup butter or margarine
1 cup coarsely chopped onion
1 cup coarsely chopped celery with leaves

1. Prepare Cooked Giblets and Broth. Set aside 1 cup chopped cooked giblets and the broth.
2. In a large bowl, toss bread cubes with the reserved chopped giblets, parsley, and a mixture of salt, thyme, rosemary, marjoram, and sage.
3. Melt butter in a skillet; add chopped onion and celery. Cook over medium heat about 5 minutes, stirring occasionally. Toss with the bread mixture.
4. Add 1 to 2 cups broth (depending upon how moist a stuffing is desired), mixing lightly until ingredients are thoroughly blended. Lightly fill body and neck cavities of turkey (do not pack).
Stuffing for a 14- to 15-pound turkey

Turkey Roasting Pan Gravy

Pan drippings
3 tablespoons flour
¼ teaspoon salt
⅛ teaspoon pepper
2 cups liquid (chicken or giblet broth, cooking liquid from potatoes, chicken bouillon, or water)
Cooked giblets, chopped (optional)

1. Remove roasted turkey from pan. Leaving brown residue in pan, pour drippings into bowl. Allow fat to rise to surface; skim off fat and reserve. Remaining juices should be reserved for use as part of liquid in gravy.
2. Measure 3 tablespoons of skimmed fat (add shortening to bring measure up to 3 tablespoons, if necessary) into roasting pan. Blend in the flour,

salt, and pepper. Stirring constantly, heat until mixture bubbles. Brown slightly, if desired.
3. Remove from heat and slowly blend in the liquid, stirring constantly.
4. Return to heat and cook rapidly, stirring constantly, until sauce thickens. While stirring, scrape bottom and sides of pan to blend in brown residue.
5. If desired, mix in chopped cooked giblets and cook until heated through. Serve hot.
About 2 cups gravy

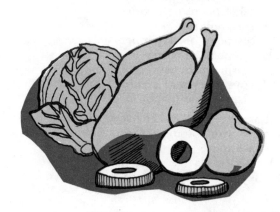

Penny-wise Chicken Casserole

1 small head cabbage, cut in 1½-inch wedges
1 teaspoon flour
1 teaspoon caraway seed
4 small tart red apples, cored and cut in ½-inch rings
2 tablespoons brown sugar
1 teaspoon flour
1 broiler-fryer, 2 to 2½ pounds, cut up
½ cup cider vinegar
1 tablespoon salt
2 tablespoons butter or margarine, melted

1. Arrange cabbage on bottom of a 2-quart shallow casserole; sprinkle with 1 teaspoon flour and the caraway seed.
2. Top with apple rings; sprinkle with a mixture of brown sugar and 1 teaspoon flour.
3. Arrange chicken pieces, skin side up, on top of cabbage-apple mixture. Pour a mixture of the vinegar and salt over chicken; pour melted butter evenly over chicken; cover casserole.
4. Bake at 350°F 45 minutes. Remove cover; bake 30 minutes or until chicken is browned and tender.
4 to 6 servings

Chicken Livers Superb

2 pounds chicken livers
¼ cup flour
1 cup finely chopped onion
½ cup butter
5 ounces fresh mushrooms, cleaned, sliced
   lengthwise through stems and caps,
   and lightly browned in butter
2 tablespoons Worcestershire sauce
2 tablespoons chili sauce
1 teaspoon salt
¼ teaspoon black pepper
½ teaspoon rosemary
½ teaspoon thyme
2 cups dairy sour cream or sour cream
   substitute (page 26)

1. Rinse and drain chicken livers. Pat free of excess moisture with absorbent paper. Coat lightly with flour. Set aside.

2. Lightly brown the onion in heated butter in a large skillet, stirring occasionally. Remove one half of onion-butter mixture and set aside for second frying of livers. Add half of the chicken livers and cook, occasionally moving and turning with a spoon, about 5 minutes, or until lightly browned. Turn into the blazer pan of a chafing dish. Fry remaining livers, using all of the onion-butter mixture; turn into the blazer pan. Set aside.

3. After browning mushrooms, blend a mixture of the Worcestershire sauce, chili sauce, salt, pepper, rosemary, and thyme with the mushrooms. Heat thoroughly.

4. Adding sour cream a small amount at a time and stirring constantly, quickly blend with mushroom mixture. Heat thoroughly (do not boil). Mix gently with livers to coat.

5. Set blazer pan over simmering water. Before serving, garnish with wreaths of **sieved hard-cooked egg white, watercress,** and **sieved hard-cooked egg yolk.** Serve with **buttered toasted English muffins.**

About 8 servings

Note: If desired, blend in ¼ cup dry sauterne or sherry with the sour cream.

HOW TO CUT UP A WHOLE BROILER-FRYER

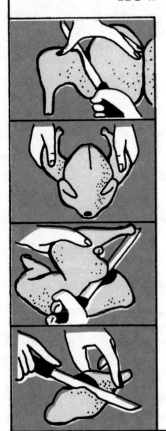

1. Cut skin between thighs and body of bird.

2. Grasp a leg of the bird in each hand and lift the bird from the table, bending its legs back as you lift. Bend legs until hip joints are free.

3. Remove legs from the body by cutting from back to front as close as possible to the backbone.

4. Remove thigh from each leg by cutting toward joint, bending, and completing cut through joint.

5. Remove each wing from body by bending it forward to show joint and cut toward joint. Break joint and complete cut.

6. Place bird on neck and cut from tail along each side of backbone through rib joints to neck. Cut skin attaching neck-and-back strip to breast. Cut neck-and-back strip in half.

7. Place the breast, skin side down, on the cutting board. Cut through the white cartilage at the V of the neck as shown.

8. Grasp breast piece firmly in both hands. Bend each side of the breast back and push up with fingers to snap out the breastbone. Cut the breast in half lengthwise.

Fried Chicken à la Southern Belle

1 broiler-fryer, 2½ to 3 pounds, cut up
1½ cups undiluted evaporated milk
1½ teaspoons savory
1 teaspoon freshly ground black pepper
¾ cup flour
1½ teaspoons paprika
1½ teaspoons salt
1 teaspoon monosodium glutamate
¼ teaspoon freshly ground black pepper
    Shortening and butter (equal parts)

1. Marinate chicken pieces 1 hour in a mixture of evaporated milk, savory, and 1 teaspoon pepper, turning once.
2. Remove chicken from milk. (Milk may be used for gravy.) Coat with a mixture of the flour, paprika, salt, monosodium glutamate, and the ¼ teaspoon pepper. Set aside 30 minutes.
3. Meanwhile, fill a large, heavy skillet one-half full with the fat. Heat to 360°F.
4. Fry only a few chicken pieces at a time 10 to 13 minutes (about 5 minutes for wings), or until tender and browned; turn pieces several times during cooking. Drain over fat a few seconds; remove to absorbent paper-lined platter. Keep warm.
5. Serve with fruit kabobs (thread **pineapple half-slices, stewed prunes,** and **maraschino cherries** onto skewers). Heat, if desired.

4 servings

Casa Chicken

1 broiler-fryer, 2 to 2½ pounds, cut up
¾ teaspoon onion salt
¾ teaspoon pepper
3 tablespoons shortening
½ cup ketchup
¼ cup soy sauce
2 tablespoons prepared mustard
½ teaspoon curry powder
2¼ cups water
2 bay leaves
2 tablespoons cornstarch
2 tablespoons water

1. Sprinkle chicken evenly with a mixture of the onion salt and pepper.
2. Heat the shortening in a large heavy skillet. Place chicken pieces, skin side down, in skillet and brown all sides.

3. Blend ketchup, soy sauce, mustard, curry powder, and water; add bay leaves. Pour mixture over chicken. Cover and cook over low heat until chicken is tender, about 45 minutes. Remove chicken to a warm serving platter.
4. If sauce is thick, add about 1 cup water and bring to boiling. Stirring constantly, gradually add a blend of cornstarch and 2 tablespoons water. Bring to boiling; cook and stir until thickened.
5. Serve with **fluffy cooked rice.** Spoon sauce over chicken and rice.

About 4 servings

Sautéed Chicken Livers

2 pounds chicken livers, rinsed and drained
1 cup milk
½ cup flour
1 teaspoon salt
¼ teaspoon white pepper
½ cup butter or margarine

1. Marinate chicken livers in milk in refrigerator overnight.
2. Drain chicken livers (reserve milk; see Note). Coat livers evenly with a mixture of the flour, salt, and pepper.
3. Heat butter in a large skillet, add livers, and cook, turning occasionally, until lightly browned.

About 6 servings

Note: The reserved milk may be thickened, seasoned, and served as gravy.

Chicken Paprika

¼ cup butter or margarine
2 tablespoons cooking oil
2 broiler-fryers, 2½ to 3 pounds each, cut up
½ cup sliced onion
½ cup sliced carrot
½ cup sliced celery
2 tablespoons paprika
3 tablespoons flour
1½ teaspoons salt
¼ teaspoon freshly ground black pepper
1 tablespoon ketchup
1¾ cups chicken broth (dissolve 2 chicken bouillon cubes in 1¾ cups boiling water)
½ cup dairy sour cream or sour cream substitute (page 26)

1. Heat half of the butter and half of the oil in a Dutch oven or large skillet. Add chicken a few pieces at a time and brown evenly; remove chicken as it browns. If needed, add more butter and oil.
2. Add any remaining butter and oil to skillet, stir in vegetables, and cook 5 minutes, stirring occasionally.
3. Stir in paprika and cook 1 minute. Blend in flour and heat until bubbly. Stir in salt, pepper, ketchup, and broth. Bring to boiling, stirring constantly and cook 1 to 2 minutes. Reduce heat and simmer, covered, 10 minutes.
4. Add chicken; simmer, covered, 35 to 40 minutes, or until chicken is tender.
5. Remove chicken and vegetables to a hot platter; keep hot.
6. Gradually add sour cream to sauce, stirring constantly; heat thoroughly (do not boil). Spoon some of the sauce over chicken; serve remaining sauce in a bowl.

6 servings

Denim Dumpling Dinner

Chicken Mixture:
2 broiler-fryer chickens (3 pounds each), rinsed
6 cups boiling water
1 tablespoon salt
1 medium onion, sliced
1½ cups cut celery (½-inch pieces)
¾ cup cut carrot (½-inch pieces)

2 cups cold water
¾ cup all-purpose flour
Dumplings:
2 packages (12 ounces each) frozen shredded hash brown potatoes, thawed
1 cup shredded sharp Cheddar cheese (about 4 ounces)
⅔ cup all-purpose flour
2 teaspoons salt
¼ teaspoon pepper
2 eggs, slightly beaten

1. Put chicken, boiling water, and salt into a saucepot. Bring to boiling, reduce heat, and simmer covered 2 to 3 hours, or until tender.
2. Remove chicken from bones, leaving in large pieces. Set aside.
3. Skim fat from broth; measure broth and add enough water to make 4 cups. Return to saucepot and add vegetables; cover and simmer until vegetables are tender, 15 to 20 minutes.
4. Add cold water to flour, stirring until well blended. Gradually add water and flour mixture to hot vegetables in saucepot, stirring constantly. Bring to boiling; simmer 3 minutes, stirring constantly. Return chicken to mixture; heat thoroughly.
5. Meanwhile, for dumplings, turn hash brown potatoes into a bowl and separate with a fork; add cheese, flour, salt, pepper, and eggs and mix with fork.
6. Put half of hot chicken mixture into each of two 13½×8¾×1¾-inch baking dishes or into one 15½×9½×2¼-inch roaster. Drop dumpling mixture by tablespoonfuls onto hot chicken mixture. Cover dishes with aluminum foil.
7. Bake at 350°F 30 minutes, or until dumplings are done.
8. Sprinkle with **snipped parsley** before serving.

About 12 servings

PASTA AND OTHER CEREAL DISHES

Easy on the budget are cereal foods such as macaroni products, rice, breadings, and cornmeal that help fill 'em up at mealtime without draining the budget.

Enriched and whole grain cereals boost the day's nourishment, too. They provide protein that's needed for body building and maintenance, especially when teamed with meat, milk, and other animal proteins. From a budget standpoint, they make a dramatic difference in the bottom line.

The variety of these "starchy" foods is vast. Cornmeal, barley, oats, rice, rye, and wheat flour each has its own distinctive taste. And by experimenting with new recipes, you can use them to provide even greater diversity.

Macaroni products come in literally dozens of forms. Everything from tiny stars to giant tubes come under this category, also called "pasta."

When buying macaroni products (which include spaghetti and noodles) look for the term "enriched" on the label. Buy the enriched form of breads and cornmeal, too. This term means that three B-vitamins and iron, removed during milling, have been returned to the product.

Rice comes in several forms, too, although not as many as pasta. You can find it as *regular milled rice* (long, medium, and short grain) which has had several layers of bran removed. It is not as nutritious as "enriched" or "parboiled" rice, to which nutrients have been added. The few pennies more for the enriched form are well spent.

Which to buy? Long-grain gives light, fluffy grains that separate well. If you are serving the rice with a meat dish, such as curry, its higher price may be justified. Shorter grains tend to clump, but this is no drawback in recipes where ingredients are molded, as in croquettes or rice rings.

Precooked rice is a convenience food. You merely heat and restore the water that has been removed after commercial cooking. You pay for this service, and some feel that the quality suffers.

Brown rice is the most nutritious form of rice, but is not as widely available as white, and takes a little longer to cook. If you can find it, try it—it has a pleasing, nutlike flavor.

Wild rice is not really a member of the rice family at all. It's the grain of a cereal grass native to America, whereas "real" rice came from Asia originally. Wild rice adds a note of luxury to any meal, and is priced accordingly, so it's not a candidate for these recipes. Neither are the packets of rice and seasonings which are better suited to those times when splurging is in order.

SOME PASTA SHAPES

Stelline

Spaghetti

Fusilli

Elbow Macaroni

Curly Lasagne

Rigatoni

Medium Egg Noodles

German Noodle Ring

1 cup medium noodles, cooked and
    drained
3 tablespoons flour
½ teaspoon salt
½ teaspoon paprika
3 tablespoons butter or margarine
1½ cups milk
6 ounces Swiss cheese, cut in pieces
2 eggs, well beaten

1. Spoon noodles into a buttered 1½-quart ring mold.
2. Blend flour, salt, and paprika into hot butter in a saucepan. Heat until bubbly. Remove from heat. Add milk gradually, stirring constantly. Bring to boiling; cook 1 to 2 minutes.
3. Remove from heat and add cheese all at one time; stir rapidly until cheese is melted. Reserve half of sauce to use later.
4. Add beaten eggs gradually to remaining sauce, blending well. Pour over noodles in mold.
5. Set mold in a pan in a 350°F oven. Pour hot water into pan to a depth of 1 inch. Bake about 40 minutes, or until mixture is set.
6. Unmold onto a large platter and pour remaining cheese sauce over mold.

About 8 servings

Tagliarini

3 tablespoons olive oil
1 pound ground beef
1½ teaspoons salt
⅛ teaspoon pepper
    Few grains cayenne pepper
1 medium-sized onion, chopped
1 clove garlic, minced
1 medium-sized green pepper, chopped
1 can (28 ounces) Italian-style tomatoes
1 can (12 ounces) whole kernel corn with
    liquid
1 can (7 ounces) pitted ripe olives, drained
½ cup olive liquid
4 ounces (about 1½ cups) medium noodles,
    uncooked
1 cup shredded sharp Cheddar cheese
    (about 4 ounces)

1. Heat olive oil in a large skillet. Brown meat in skillet. Add salt and peppers, onion, garlic, and

green pepper; cook, stirring frequently, until onion is soft.
2. Add remaining ingredients except cheese; stir to blend well. Cover closely and cook over low heat about 35 minutes, or until noodles are tender; stir occasionally.
3. Before serving, blend in cheese and heat only until cheese is melted.

8 to 10 servings

Rice Pilaf

6 tablespoons olive oil
¼ cup finely chopped onion
2 cups uncooked long grain rice
4 cups well-seasoned chicken broth
1½ teaspoons salt
½ cup shredded Cheddar cheese or
    pasteurized process cheese (about 2
    ounces)

1. Heat oil in a large heavy skillet having a heat-resistant handle. Add onion and rice; cook over low heat 3 minutes, or until rice is golden.
2. Add chicken broth and salt; cover tightly.
3. Bake at 375°F 35 to 40 minutes. Remove from oven; fluff rice with a fork and stir in cheese.

8 servings

Cheeseroni Casserole

7 ounces elbow macaroni, cooked and
    drained
2 cups shredded sharp Cheddar cheese or
    pasteurized process cheese (about 8
    ounces)
1 teaspoon salt
¼ teaspoon pepper
⅛ teaspoon oregano, crushed
1 small onion, thinly sliced and separated
    in rings
1⅔ cups (13-ounce can) evaporated milk
2 tablespoons shredded Parmesan cheese
1 medium-sized ripe tomato, cut in eight
    wedges

1. Using half of each at a time, layer the following ingredients in a buttered 2-quart casserole: macaroni, Cheddar cheese, a mixture of salt, pepper, and oregano, onion rings, and evaporated milk. Sprinkle Parmesan cheese over top.
2. Heat in a 350°F oven about 20 minutes. Arrange tomato wedges on top and heat 10 minutes.

6 to 8 servings

Denim Dumpling Dinner;
Patchwork Casserole;
Frozen Lemon Velvet

Ground Beef-Noodle Scallop

- 2 to 3 tablespoons shortening
- 2 cups chopped onion
- 2 pounds ground beef
- 1 can (4 ounces) sliced mushrooms, drained
- 1 can (about 10 ounces) condensed cream of chicken soup
- 1¼ cups milk
- 2 teaspoons salt
- ¼ teaspoon pepper
- ¼ cup soy sauce
- 1 teaspoon Worcestershire sauce
- 8 ounces fine noodles, cooked and drained
- 2 cups shredded sharp Cheddar cheese (about 8 ounces)

1. Heat shortening in a large skillet. Add the onion and cook about 5 minutes, turning occasionally with a spoon. Add the meat and separate into pieces. Cook until meat is browned and onion is tender.
2. Combine mushrooms and soup. Add the milk gradually, stirring until smooth. Blend in the salt, pepper, soy sauce, and Worcestershire sauce. Stir into meat mixture in skillet and cook until heated thoroughly.
3. Turn cooked noodles into a 3-quart shallow baking dish. Spread the meat-soup mixture over the noodles. Top with the shredded cheese.
4. Heat in a 350°F oven 15 minutes.

About 10 servings

Turkey-Tomato Mac

- 1 tablespoon vegetable oil
- 1¼ cups minced onion
- 1 miniature green cherry pepper, seeds removed and pepper minced
- 1 miniature red pepper, seeds removed and pepper minced
- 3 small cloves garlic, minced
- 1 tablespoon sugar
- ½ teaspoon basil, crushed
- 1 can (28 ounces) Italian-style tomatoes
- 1 can (6 ounces) tomato paste
  Salt and freshly ground pepper
- 8 ounces macaroni or spaghetti, broken
  Butter or margarine, melted
- 3 cups shredded extra sharp Cheddar cheese or sharp pasteurized process American cheese (about 12 ounces)
  Roast turkey or chicken, sliced or cut in bite-size pieces

1. Heat oil in a large skillet. Add onion, peppers, and garlic. Cook until tender, stirring occasionally. Stir in sugar, basil, tomatoes, and tomato paste; season to taste with salt and pepper. Cover and simmer 30 minutes.
2. Meanwhile, cook macaroni according to package directions; drain. Toss with desired amount of melted butter and half of the cheese.
3. Spoon a small amount of the sauce onto the bottom of a 2-quart shallow casserole. Add half the cooked macaroni and half the turkey, then spoon half the sauce over turkey. Repeat layering, ending with sauce. Sprinkle remaining cheese over top.
4. Set in a 325°F oven until thoroughly heated.

6 to 8 servings

Fried Rice

- ¾ cup uncooked rice
- 2 tablespoons very finely chopped fresh mushrooms
- ¼ to ½ teaspoon grated onion
- 2 tablespoons butter
- 2½ cups chicken broth (dissolve 3 chicken bouillon cubes in 2½ cups boiling water)
- 1 tablespoon finely chopped carrot
- 1 tablespoon finely chopped green pepper

1. Add rice, mushrooms, and onion to hot butter in a large heavy skillet; cook until golden brown.
2. Stir broth into rice mixture. Cover and cook over low heat 30 minutes, or until rice is tender.
3. Add carrot and green pepper and toss lightly.

About 8 servings

Beef Sirloin Tip Roast
with Parmesan Barbecue Baste;
Italian Potato Salad

Sweet Potato-Rice Casserole

1½ cups coarsely chopped celery
1½ cups chopped onion
 2 cups rice
 ½ cup butter or margarine
2½ cups chicken broth
 2 tablespoons brown sugar
1¾ teaspoons salt
 ½ teaspoon black pepper
 1 teaspoon ground coriander
 ¾ teaspoon crushed rosemary
 ¼ teaspoon ground ginger
 2 eggs, slightly beaten
 1 can (18 ounces) vacuum-packed sweet
    potatoes, cut in ½-inch pieces

1. Stir celery, onion, and rice into hot butter in a large heavy skillet; cook over low heat until rice is golden yellow, stirring occasionally.
2. Stir in 2 cups of the chicken broth and a mixture of brown sugar, salt, pepper, coriander, rosemary, and ginger. Cover skillet; bring mixture to boiling and cook over low heat 15 minutes, or until rice is tender; cool.
3. Mix eggs with remaining ½ cup chicken broth; blend into the rice mixture. Add sweet potatoes and toss lightly. Turn into a greased 2-quart shallow baking dish.
4. Heat in a 325°F oven 20 to 25 minutes.

About 8 servings

Ham 'n' Chicken Specialty

 6 green onions with tops, finely chopped
 1 stalk celery, sliced lengthwise
 ¼ cup margarine
1½ cups cooked ham pieces
 1 cup cooked chicken pieces
 1 teaspoon salt
 ½ teaspoon pepper
 1 cup dairy sour cream or sour cream
    substitute (page 26)
 1 cup creamed cottage cheese
1½ cups thin spaghetti pieces (1½ inches),
    cooked and drained
 1 cup shredded sharp Cheddar cheese or
    pasteurized process cheese (about 4
    ounces)

1. Cook green onion and celery until just tender in hot margarine in a large skillet or saucepan. Mix in ham, chicken, and a mixture of salt, pepper, and celery salt; heat thoroughly.
2. Blend sour cream and cottage cheese. Add to spaghetti and toss lightly until thoroughly mixed. Add ham mixture and toss lightly.
3. Turn into buttered 1½-quart casserole or baking dish. Top evenly with shredded cheese.
4. Broil 3 inches from source of heat about 15 minutes, or until mixture is bubbly and cheese is delicately browned. Garnish with **parsley**.

About 6 servings

Garlic-Buttered Fusilli

 5 tablespoons butter
 1 clove garlic
 8 ounces fusilli, cooked and drained
    Finely snipped parsley

1. Heat butter and garlic in a small skillet.
2. Pour garlic butter over cooked fusilli, add a generous amount of parsley, and toss until mixed.

About 6 servings

Spaghetti Casserole

 1 onion
 1 large green pepper
 1 cup pimento-stuffed olives
 8 ounces spaghetti, cooked and drained
 1 can (16 ounces) tomatoes
 1 pound fresh mushrooms, sliced
    lengthwise
 2 cups shredded sharp Cheddar cheese
    (about 8 ounces)
    Bread crumbs
 ¼ cup butter
 ½ cup milk or half-and-half

1. Put onion, green pepper, and olives through meat grinder. Mix with spaghetti, tomatoes, and mushrooms. Season to taste with **salt** and **pepper**.
2. Turn into a greased 2½-quart casserole. Sprinkle with cheese and bread crumbs. Dot with butter. Pour cream over top.
3. Bake at 350°F 1½ hours.

6 to 8 servings

EGG AND CHEESE DISHES

Eggs and cheese prove the old saying that good things come in small packages. Few other foods pack so much protein and other nourishment into such compact form.

And since both offer complete protein (the kind from an animal source) they can be teamed with protein from a vegetable source (such as that in macaroni and rice) to produce economical, nutritious dishes.

EGGS

Freshness is the primary concern of the egg buyer. It may help to know that freshness does not depend so much on how long it's been since the egg was laid as on how it's been handled in the meantime.

An egg that was laid two or three weeks ago and handled properly may be fresher than yesterday's egg that hasn't been refrigerated. Never buy eggs from an unrefrigerated counter, no matter how low the price. And it follows that you should put eggs in the refrigerator as soon as you get home from the store.

EGG GRADES

Eggs are graded from high to low—AA, A, B, and C—and prices conform to grade. The AA egg has a yolk that is well centered and a white that is firm. This grade makes the most attractive fried or poached eggs, and the whites, when beaten, give the biggest volume of all grades. Grade A performs well for these uses, too—it is just slightly less showy than the AA.

B and C grade eggs are usually processed for use in dried and frozen food; you are unlikely to find them in the store.

EGG SIZES

The size of eggs is based on the weight of a dozen eggs.

Size	Weight per dozen
Jumbo	30 ounces
Extra Large	27 ounces
Large	24 ounces
Medium	21 ounces
Small	18 ounces

Most recipes are designed for use with large or medium eggs, so either size will work well in cooking. Extra large and jumbo make an impressive appearance as fried or poached eggs, where the generous size makes a difference. Small eggs may be sufficient for children or dieters.

COLOR

The color of the shell has no bearing on the quality of the eggs, but in some localities brown are favored over white, and elsewhere, just the opposite. Chances are, you'll find only the favored shade in the area where you live.

On rare occasions, you will find a blood spot in an egg. While unattractive, it does not detract from the food value or wholesomeness of the egg. If you use the egg as an ingredient in a baked recipe, you won't notice it.

BUYING EGGS

Be sure to check the carton before you buy to make sure there are no cracked eggs. If an egg is accidentally cracked after you buy it, cook it very well before serving. It is possible for bacteria to enter the cracked shell.

The shopper who is willing to do a little mental arithmetic can find the best buy in the egg case. Large eggs give 12½ percent more volume than medium eggs, so if they are priced 10 percent higher, they are clearly the better buy.

For example, if the price of medium eggs is 60 cents, 10 percent is 6 cents. If large eggs are 66 cents, they are the better bargain.

CHEESE

When buying cheese, it helps to know the distinction between natural and process cheese.

NATURAL CHEESE

This is made directly from the curd of milk and not reprocessed or blended. Many natural cheeses are made from unpasteurized milk.

Natural cheeses are either unripened (sometimes called uncured or fresh) or ripened (cured). Unripened varieties are cream or cottage cheeses. Ripened cheese includes a whole array of cheeses ranging from the relatively mild Cheddar to the robust Roquefort. During ripening, microorganisms act to develop flavor and other characteristics of the individual cheese.

Domestic natural cheeses are generally less expensive than imported ones. The quality and price of both are higher as a rule than process cheese.

PROCESS CHEESE

A large proportion of the cheese made in this country is process cheese. It is made by grinding and mixing together one or more natural cheeses with the application of heat and an emulsifying agent. Pasteurization stops further enzyme action, so no ripening takes place. This category of cheese includes process cheese food (available in slices, rolls, links, and loaves), process cheese spread (in jars or small, soft loaves), cold-pack cheese prepared by grinding and blending natural cheeses, and cold-pack cheese food which includes skim milk or whey solids.

MEASURING CHEESE FOR RECIPES

A handy rule of thumb to remember for figuring weights of cheese for recipes is this: One cup of shredded cheese equals about 4 ounces. And of course, it's cheaper to shred your own than to buy preshredded cheese.

Poached Eggs

Grease bottom of a skillet. Pour in **water** to a depth of 2 inches. Bring water to boiling; reduce heat to keep water at simmering point. Break each **egg** into a saucer or small dish and quickly slip into water, holding the saucer close to the surface of the water. Cook 3 to 5 minutes, depending upon firmness desired. Carefully remove egg with a slotted spoon or pancake turner. Drain by holding spoon on absorbent paper for a few seconds. Season with **salt** and **pepper**. Serve immediately.

Scrambled Eggs

    6 eggs
    6 tablespoons milk, cream, or undiluted
       evaporated milk
    ¾ teaspoon salt
    ⅛ teaspoon pepper
    3 tablespoons butter or margarine

1. Beat the eggs, milk, salt, and pepper together until blended.
2. Heat an 8- or 10-inch skillet until hot enough to sizzle a drop of water. Melt butter in skillet.
3. Pour egg mixture into skillet and cook over low heat. With a spatula, lift mixture from bottom and sides of skillet as it thickens, allowing uncooked portion to flow to bottom. Cook until eggs are thick and creamy.

4 servings

Scrambled Eggs Deluxe

Follow recipe for Scrambled Eggs. Add **½ teaspoon Worcestershire sauce** and **¼ cup finely shredded Cheddar cheese** to egg mixture in skillet. Cook as directed. Before removing from heat, gently stir in **1 medium-sized firm ripe tomato**, cut in small cubes, and **1 cup croutons**, ¼ to ½ inch.

4 to 6 servings

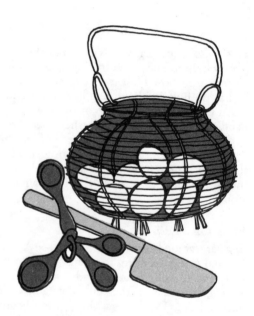

French Omelet

    6 eggs
    6 tablespoons milk or water
    ¾ teaspoon salt
    ⅛ teaspoon black pepper
    3 tablespoons butter or margarine

1. Beat the eggs, milk, salt, and pepper together until blended.
2. Heat an 8- to 10-inch skillet until just hot enough to sizzle a drop of water; melt butter in the skillet.
3. Pour egg mixture into skillet. As edges of omelet begin to thicken, draw cooked portions toward center with spoon or fork to allow un-

cooked mixture to flow to bottom of skillet, tilting skillet as necessary; do not stir.

4. When eggs are thickened but surface is still moist, increase heat to quickly brown the bottom of omelet. Loosen edges carefully and fold in half; slide onto a warm serving platter. If desired, garnish with sprigs of parsley.

4 to 6 servings

Citrus Omelet

Follow recipe for French Omelet. Substitute **3 tablespoons lemon or orange juice** and **3 tablespoons water** for liquid.

Chicken Liver Omelet

Follow recipe for French Omelet. Just before serving, enclose in omelet **¼ pound chicken livers** which have been coated with **seasoned flour** and browned in **butter or margarine** with **minced onion**.

Bacon Omelet

Unwrap **½ pound sliced bacon**, do not separate, and cut crosswise into fine thin strips. Put into an unheated 8- to 10-inch skillet and fry until crisp. Drain bacon fat from skillet and return about 2 tablespoons fat to skillet. Follow recipe for French Omelet. Decrease salt to ½ teaspoon, omit butter, and pour egg mixture over bacon in skillet.

Eggs Florentine à l'Orange

1 tablespoon butter or margarine
½ cup chopped onion
¼ pound mushrooms, cleaned and sliced
1 package (10 ounces) frozen chopped spinach, thawed and drained
1 teaspoon salt
⅛ teaspoon pepper
1 cup Florida orange sections*
4 eggs
  Salt and pepper

1. Melt butter in medium saucepan. Add onion and cook until tender; add mushrooms and cook 5 minutes. Stir in spinach, salt, pepper, and orange sections.

2. Divide equally among 4 buttered ramekins or individual shallow baking dishes, making a depression in the center of each.

3. Bake in a 350°F oven 15 to 20 minutes, or until hot.

4. Add 1 egg to the depression in each dish; sprinkle with additional salt and pepper. Bake 7 to 10 minutes longer, or until egg white is set.

4 servings

*To section Florida oranges, cut off peel round and round spiral fashion. Go over fruit again, removing any remaining white membrane. Cut along side of each dividing membrane from outside to middle of core. Remove section by section over a bowl; reserve juice for other use.

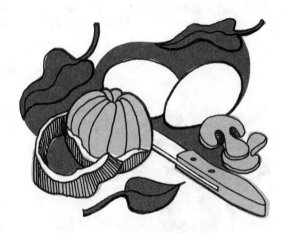

Shirred Eggs with Sausage and Cheese

Salami or bologna, thinly sliced
2 tablespoons butter or margarine
  Swiss or Cheddar cheese, thinly sliced
6 eggs

1. Brown salami lightly in the butter in a skillet; reserve drippings in skillet.

2. Line a 9-inch pie plate with salami and add an even layer of cheese.

3. Break and slip eggs, one at a time, onto the cheese. Pour drippings over all. Season with **salt** and **pepper** and drizzle with **Worcestershire sauce**.

4. Bake at 325°F about 22 minutes, or until eggs are as firm as desired. Serve immediately with **parsley-buttered toast**.

6 servings

Mushroom Cheese Sauce on Toast

2 cups shredded Cheddar or pasteurized process American cheese (about 8 ounces)
2 tablespoons flour
¼ teaspoon paprika
1 can (about 10 ounces) condensed golden mushroom soup
½ cup water
Toast slices

1. Toss together cheese, flour, and paprika.
2. Combine soup and water in a 2-quart saucepan. Heat until bubbly over medium heat.
3. Add cheese mixture, ½ cup at a time, and stir until well combined after each addition. Heat until cheese is melted.
4. Serve over toast slices.

About 4 servings

Cheese Strata

12 slices white bread, crusts removed
Butter or margarine, softened
4 cups shredded Cheddar cheese (about 1 pound)
5 eggs
3 cups milk
2½ teaspoons salt
¼ teaspoon pepper
¾ teaspoon dry mustard

1. Spread both sides of bread slices with softened butter. Place half of the bread in one layer in a greased 13×9×2-inch (3-quart) baking dish; reserve remainder.
2. Sprinkle shredded cheese evenly over bread.
3. Cover with remaining bread slices and the remainder of the cheese.
4. Beat remaining ingredients together until frothy and blended. Pour over all. Let stand 1 hour.
5. Bake at 325°F for 45 minutes, or until puffed and browned.

About 8 servings

Swiss and Tuna Pie

3 eggs
½ teaspoon salt
½ teaspoon dry mustard
Few grains cayenne pepper
1½ cups half-and-half
1 unbaked 9-inch pastry shell (see page 19), chilled
2 cans (6½ or 7 ounces each) tuna, drained and flaked
2 cups shredded Swiss cheese (about 8 ounces)
1 tablespoon flour

1. Beat eggs, salt, dry mustard, and cayenne pepper together until foamy. Beat in half-and-half.
2. Cover bottom of pastry shell with a layer of tuna. Sprinkle half of the cheese over the tuna. Repeat layering. Sprinkle flour over cheese. Pour egg mixture over all.
3. Bake at 425°F 15 minutes. Reduce oven temperature to 300°F and bake 25 minutes, or until a knife inserted halfway between center and edge of filling comes out clean.

4 to 6 servings

Cheese Soufflé

¼ cup flour
¾ teaspoon salt
¾ teaspoon monosodium glutamate
½ teaspoon dry mustard
⅛ teaspoon paprika
1⅔ cups (13-ounce can) evaporated milk
¼ teaspoon Tabasco
2 cups coarsely shredded sharp Cheddar cheese (about 8 ounces)
6 egg yolks, well beaten
6 egg whites

1. Blend the flour, salt, monosodium glutamate, dry mustard, and paprika in a heavy saucepan. Add

the evaporated milk gradually, then the Tabasco, stirring until smooth. Bring to boiling; stir and cook 1 to 2 minutes.

2. Add cheese all at one time and stir until cheese is melted. Remove from heat.

3. Pour sauce slowly into beaten egg yolks, beating constantly.

4. Beat egg whites until stiff, not dry, peaks are formed. Spoon the sauce over egg whites and fold together until just blended. Turn into an ungreased 2-quart soufflé dish (deep casserole with straight sides). About 1½ inches from edge of dish, draw a circle by inserting the tip of a spoon 1 inch into the mixture to form a "top hat."

5. Bake at 300°F 55 to 60 minutes, or until a knife inserted halfway between center and edge of soufflé comes out clean.

About 6 servings

Welsh Rabbit in Chafing Dish

¼ cup butter
8 cups shredded sharp Cheddar cheese (about 2 pounds)
2 teaspoons Worcestershire sauce
1 teaspoon dry mustard
Few grains cayenne pepper
4 eggs, slightly beaten
1 cup light cream or half-and-half

1. In a chafing dish blazer over simmering water, melt butter. Add cheese and heat, stirring occasionally, until cheese is melted. Mix in Worcestershire sauce, dry mustard, and cayenne pepper.

2. Blend eggs and cream; strain. Mix into melted cheese. Cook until thick, stirring frequently.

3. Garnish with **parsley sprigs**. Serve over toasted **English muffin halves**.

6 cups Welsh Rabbit

Note: When reheating mixture, thin with desired amount of **milk**.

Cheese-Onion Pie

1 tablespoon bacon drippings or shortening
1 cup chopped onion
2 cups shredded cheese (about 8 ounces)
1 unbaked 9-inch pie shell (see page 19)
3 eggs, slightly beaten

¾ cup dairy sour cream or sour cream substitute (page 26)
½ teaspoon salt
Dash pepper

1. Using bacon drippings or shortening, stir-fry chopped onion until tender.

2. In bottom of pie shell, spread onion and shredded cheese.

3. Combine beaten eggs, sour cream, salt, and pepper in mixing bowl. Pour over onion-cheese mixture in pie shell.

4. Bake at 375°F 25 to 30 minutes, or until center is set. Do not overbake.

One 9-inch pie

Parsleyed Cheese Puff

1 cup milk
1½ teaspoons celery salt
3 cups soft ¼-inch bread cubes
2 cups shredded Cheddar cheese (about 8 ounces)
½ cup finely snipped parsley
4 egg yolks, well beaten
4 egg whites

1. Heat milk and celery salt over low heat until just hot.

2. Pour milk into a large bowl; immediately add bread cubes, cheese, and parsley; mix lightly.

3. Add beaten egg yolks and gently fold together.

4. Beat egg whites until stiff, not dry, peaks are formed. Gently fold with cheese mixture. Turn into a buttered 1½-quart casserole.

5. Bake at 325°F about 55 minutes, or until set. Garnish with **snipped parsley**.

About 6 servings

FRUITS AND VEGETABLES

FRESH PRODUCE

The best tip for saving money on fruits and vegetables is "Grow your own!" But unless you happen to have a large yard and a lot of free time (or you're a farmer), it's pretty hard to manage. Next best suggestion is to find a store that sells consistently high-quality produce at reasonable prices.

Fruits and vegetables served raw are good for you and make light work. In cooking, some nutrients are lost and some of the good-for-you fiber breaks down. So get in the habit of serving produce *au naturel*—in salads, as crisp accompaniments to a meal, as edible garnish, and as out-of-hand desserts.

But when you cook fruits and vegetables, keep it to a minimum. The U.S. Department of Agriculture calls these the "Three R's" of produce cookery:

Reduce amount of cooking water.

Reduce length of cooking time.

Reduce the amount of surface area exposed. This means cooking vegetables whole or in large pieces rather than minced or grated, which allows more cut surfaces to spill out nutrients.

Fresh fruits and vegetables often cost a little more than their processed counterparts, but they offer quality that many people feel can't be matched. Whether or not they offer more nutrients is debatable. Canned and frozen items are picked when the food is at its nutritious best, and processed by methods designed to conserve nutrients. How food is handled at home (cooking, serving, and storing) will have a great influence on how well food value is retained. Food that is overcooked or mishandled will lose nutrients, regardless of the form in which it was purchased.

When planning meals, try to include a citrus fruit every day, and a dark green or deep yellow fruit or vegetable every other day.

CANNED FRUITS AND VEGETABLES

All canned foods are *cooked* foods; they need the briefest of heating before you serve them. In fact, the shorter the heating period, the more of their natural quality you will capture.

To keep canned foods as fresh-seeming as possible, drain the liquid from the opened can into a saucepan. Bring it to boiling, add the vegetable, and cook only until heated through. In this way, foods that have natural firmness, such as beans, will retain more of their "snap."

Users of canned foods sometimes notice a mottled look, spots, or an etched pattern inside the can, particularly with acid foods such as tomatoes. That results from the action of the acid on the tin lining. It has no effect on the wholesomeness of the food, which is perfectly safe to eat.

Dark blue, brown, or black marks on the lining of a can sometimes result when the food releases sulfur during canning. This is a natural process and the food is safe to eat.

On the other hand, if you find a can completely blackened on the inside, the tin plating has been removed. The can is probably very old and should be discarded.

Don't avoid cans with small bumps, but deep creases are something else. Deep dents could mean that a seam is broken and air may have reached the inside of the can. No matter how low the price tag, don't buy!

FROZEN FRUITS AND VEGETABLES

Surprising as it may sound, commercially frozen foods may deliver more vitamins and minerals than their fresh counterparts. This is because they are usually quick-frozen before there is an opportunity for nutrient loss.

"Pour and store" packages, either poly-bags or cartons, usually offer the most economical way to buy frozen foods. Use only what you need at a given meal; then return the rest to the freezer, still frozen, for later use.

When buying, choose frozen packages that are firm and clean. Discoloration from the contents means that the food has thawed and been refrozen. Recognize other signs of defrosting such as sweating and ice-coated, wet, or limp packages. While the contents might be safe to eat, there could be a quality loss.

At the checkout counter, ask that your frozen foods be packed in an extra bag if there will be a delay in getting them into the freezer. Once home, put the frozen items away immediately, and store them at 0°F. Storage periods vary for different foods (see the chart on page 90). The storage period in a one-door refrigerator-freezer combination, or in the ice-cube section of an older refrigerator, will be shorter than in a separate freezer or freezer compartment.

Lancaster County Lima Beans

1 pound fresh lima beans (or frozen)
4 large potatoes, pared and diced
2 cups milk
2 tablespoons butter or margarine
1½ teaspoons salt
⅛ teaspoon pepper

1. Partially cook lima beans in boiling water 10 minutes in covered saucepan. Add potatoes and cook 15 minutes longer, or until vegetables are tender. Drain.
2. Add milk, butter, salt, and pepper to vegetables in saucepan; stir gently. Heat thoroughly.

About 10 servings

Buckaroo Beans

1 pound dried pinto or red beans
6 cups water
2 medium-sized onions, thinly sliced
2 large cloves garlic, thinly sliced
1 small bay leaf
1 teaspoon salt
½ pound salt pork, slab bacon, or smoked ham
1 can (16 ounces) whole tomatoes
½ cup coarsely chopped green pepper
2 tablespoons brown sugar
2 teaspoons chili powder
½ teaspoon dry mustard
¼ teaspoon crushed oregano or cumin

1. Wash beans, drain, and place in heavy kettle or saucepot with the water; bring rapidly to boiling. Boil 2 minutes and remove from heat. Set aside covered 1 hour. (If desired, pour the water over the washed beans in kettle, cover, and let stand overnight. Do not drain.)
2. Stir in the onion, garlic, bay leaf, and salt. (If salt pork is used, add salt later.)
3. Wash salt pork thoroughly. Slice through pork or bacon twice each way, not quite to the rind. Cut ham into ½-inch cubes, if used. Add meat to beans and bring rapidly to boiling. (To prevent foam from forming, add 1 **tablespoon butter or margarine**.) Cover tightly and cook slowly about 1½ hours.
4. Stir in tomatoes, green pepper, and a mixture of the remaining ingredients. Bring rapidly to boiling and reduce heat. Season to taste with **salt** and simmer, covered, 6 hours or longer; remove cover the last hour of cooking, if desired. If necessary, gently stir beans occasionally to prevent sticking on bottom of kettle. There should be just enough liquid remaining on beans to resemble a medium-thick sauce.
5. Serving piping hot in soup plates.

About 6 servings

Company Cabbage

5 cups finely shredded cabbage
1 cup finely shredded carrot
½ cup chopped green onion
½ teaspoon salt
⅛ teaspoon pepper
1 beef bouillon cube
¼ cup boiling water
1 teaspoon prepared mustard
⅓ cup chopped pecans
¼ cup butter or margarine
¼ teaspoon paprika

1. Combine cabbage, carrot, onion, salt, and pepper in a large, heavy saucepan.
2. Dissolve bouillon cube in boiling water and add to vegetables in saucepan; toss with fork to blend thoroughly. Cover tightly and cook over low heat 5 minutes; stir once during cooking. Drain if necessary. Turn into a warm serving dish. Keep hot.
3. Stir mustard and pecans into hot butter in a small saucepan and heat thoroughly. Pour over vegetables. Sprinkle with paprika.

6 servings

Stuffed Peppers

    4 large green peppers
    ½ cup butter or margarine
    2 cups diced ham or 1 pound ground beef
    1 cup cooked rice
    2 tablespoons minced onion
    ¼ teaspoon dry mustard
    ¼ teaspoon garlic salt
    ⅛ teaspoon pepper
    1½ cups tomato juice
    4 ounces Cheddar cheese, cut in 8 slices

1. Cut green peppers into halves lengthwise; remove and discard white fiber and seeds. Drop pepper halves into boiling **salted water**; simmer 5 minutes. Remove and invert to drain.
2. Heat butter in a saucepan. Add ham and toss lightly with a fork. (If using ground beef, omit butter and cook until all pink color is gone.) Mix in rice, onion, dry mustard, garlic salt, and pepper.
3. Pour tomato juice into a 2-quart shallow baking dish.
4. Spoon filling into pepper halves, heaping slightly. Place a slice of cheese on top of each filled pepper and set peppers in baking dish.
5. Bake at 350°F about 20 minutes. Increase temperature to 400°F and bake 10 minutes, or until cheese is lightly browned.
6. Spoon tomato juice over peppers before serving.

4 servings

Hi-Style Spinach

    2 packages (10 ounces each) frozen
        chopped spinach
    ¼ cup water
    3 slices white bread (crusts removed), cut
        in ½-inch cubes
    ⅓ cup butter or margarine
    1½ teaspoons Worcestershire sauce
    1 teaspoon grated onion
    ½ clove garlic, minced
    ½ teaspoon seasoned salt
    3 tablespoons butter or margarine, melted
    1 cup coarse fresh bread crumbs
    ⅓ cup shredded Parmesan cheese

1. Heat spinach with water only until thawed. Remove from heat (do not drain) and mix in the bread cubes, ⅓ cup butter, Worcestershire sauce, onion, garlic, and seasoned salt. Bring to boiling, reduce heat, and simmer 10 minutes.
2. Turn mixture into an 8-inch square pan.

3. Toss 3 tablespoons butter with crumbs and cheese; sprinkle over top.
4. Heat in a 400°F oven 10 to 12 minutes, or until crumbs are golden brown.

6 to 8 servings

Italian Potato Salad

    1 package (2 pounds) frozen southern-style
        hash brown potatoes
    1 package (9 ounces) frozen Italian green
        beans
    1 teaspoon seasoned salt
    ¼ teaspoon pepper
    ⅔ cup bottled creamy Italian dressing
    ½ cup chopped celery
    ½ cup pitted ripe olives, cut in half
        crosswise
    2 hard-cooked eggs, diced
    2 tablespoons chopped green onion
    ½ teaspoon salt
    1 cup cherry tomatoes, cut in half
    1 cup shredded Provolone cheese (about 4
        ounces)
    Romaine leaves

1. Thaw hash brown potatoes.
2. Cook Italian green beans, following package directions, until just tender; drain.
3. Combine potatoes and beans in a bowl. Sprinkle with seasoned salt and pepper. Chill.
4. Combine dressing, celery, olives, eggs, onion, and salt in a large bowl. Add chilled vegetables and toss to coat with dressing. Lightly mix in tomatoes and cheese. Chill thoroughly to blend flavors, at least several hours.
5. To serve, spoon salad into a bowl lined with romaine.

About 10 servings

Tart Cabbage Slaw

    2½ tablespoons cider vinegar
    1 teaspoon grated onion
    1 tablespoon sugar
    1 teaspoon salt
    ⅛ teaspoon pepper
    3 cups finely shredded cabbage

Combine vinegar, onion, sugar, salt, and pepper. Pour over shredded cabbage and toss lightly.

6 servings

Carrots Lyonnaise

2 tablespoons butter or margarine
3 cups (about 1 pound) thinly sliced carrots
¼ cup chopped onion
1 teaspoon sugar
¼ teaspoon thyme
¼ teaspoon salt
Few grains pepper

1. Heat butter in a saucepan. Add carrots and remaining ingredients.
2. Cover and cook over medium heat about 15 minutes, or until carrots are tender; stir occasionally..

About 4 servings

O'Brien Potatoes

6 or 7 medium potatoes, cooked and peeled
3 to 4 tablespoons fat
¼ cup chopped onion
¼ cup minced green pepper
2 tablespoons minced pimento
⅓ cup milk
1 teaspoon salt
¼ teaspoon pepper
¼ teaspoon paprika

1. Dice or coarsely chop the potatoes; set aside.
2. Heat the fat in a large skillet. Mix in the onion, green pepper, pimento, and potatoes. Add the milk and sprinkle with a blend of seasonings. Cook, stirring frequently, until potatoes are lightly browned.
3. Turn into a heated serving dish and garnish with **parsley sprigs**.

6 servings

Fried Green Pepper Strips

2 large green peppers
½ cup fine dry bread crumbs
⅓ cup grated Parmesan cheese
1½ teaspoons salt
⅛ teaspoon pepper
1 egg, fork beaten
2 tablespoons water
Fat for frying

1. Clean green peppers and cut into ⅛-inch rings. Cut each ring into halves or thirds.

2. Coat with a mixture of bread crumbs, cheese, salt, and pepper. Dip into a mixture of egg and water. Coat again with crumb mixture. Chill 1 hour.
3. Heat a ½-inch layer of fat to 375°F in a skillet. Cover surface with chilled green pepper strips. Fry about 30 seconds, or until golden brown. Remove strips with fork or slotted spoon. Drain on absorbent paper.

4 servings

Glazed Onions

2 tablespoons brown sugar
¼ cup margarine
8 small onions (about 1 pound) peeled, cooked, and dried

Blend brown sugar into hot margarine in a skillet and stir until sugar is dissolved. Add cooked onions to skillet and turn several times to glaze evenly.

4 servings

Broccoli with Horseradish Cream

½ teaspoon prepared horseradish
½ teaspoon prepared mustard
⅛ teaspoon salt
¾ cup dairy sour cream or sour cream substitute (page 26)
2 pounds broccoli, cooked and drained

Blend horseradish, mustard, salt, and sour cream in a small saucepan. Heat just until hot. Pour over hot broccoli.

About 4 servings

TREATS

America has an oversized sweet tooth. Each of us in this country puts away over one hundred pounds of sugar each year! This amount could be cut considerably with no loss to nutrition, and to the everlasting benefit of the food budget, calorie count, and the dentist's bill.

But we're in the habit of thinking "sweets" for "snacks." Sugar coating seems to make everything more palatable, just as the teaspoon of sugar helps the medicine go down.

It won't be easy, but perhaps the prospect of lower food costs and fewer trips to the dentist will provide the incentive to seek out some alternatives to sugary sweets.

This doesn't mean avoiding sugar entirely. You wouldn't find that practical, unless a medical problem required it. Some sugar is needed to give the flavor and texture we prize in many baked goods; including such un-sweet items as breads.

Instead, get acquainted with the sources of natural sugar for snacks and desserts. A fruit bowl does double duty as centerpiece and dessert, saving money and work while reducing sugar intake. Add a slice of cheese and you have a classic continental dessert.

You can still let them eat cake, but forego the gooey frosting. Instead, give it a light dusting of confectioners' sugar. Or prick the top of a sponge cake and sprinkle on a mixture of orange juice and confectioners' sugar.

The after-school crowd is ravenous for snacks. They will grab whatever is handy, so make sure they find nutritious nibbles. Peanut butter (from the big economy jar) on bread or crackers is filling, and vegetables such as carrots and celery, cut into strips, are fun to munch.

Pop is expensive; homemade iced tea offers just as much refreshment for a fraction of the cost. Fruit drinks often cost less than carbonated drinks and contribute nutrients, too.

A habit is hard to break—especially when it means giving up something as enjoyable as eating sweets. The answer is to find alternatives with enough appeal to make up for the loss. Then you'll get a double reward—good eating along with the lower food bill.

Snacks

Cottage Cheese Rolls

¼ cup warm orange juice (105° to 115°F)
1 package active dry yeast
1 cup (8 ounces) creamed cottage cheese
2 teaspoons caraway seed
1 tablespoon sugar
1 teaspoon grated orange peel
1 tablespoon grated onion
1 teaspoon salt
¼ teaspoon baking soda
1 egg, slightly beaten
2⅓ cups sifted all-purpose flour

1. Put orange juice into a warm large bowl. Sprinkle yeast over orange juice and stir until dissolved.
2. Heat cottage cheese in a small saucepan just until lukewarm. Stir cheese into yeast mixture. Add remaining ingredients except flour; mix well. Beat in flour gradually until completely blended, scraping down sides of bowl as necessary; beat vigorously about 20 strokes (dough will be sticky and heavy).
3. Cover bowl with a clean towel; let rise in a warm place about 1 hour, or until double in bulk.
4. Stir dough down. Divide evenly among 12 greased 2½-inch muffin pan wells. Cover with towel; let rise again 35 minutes, or until double in bulk.
5. Bake at 350°F 25 minutes, or until rolls are golden brown and sound hollow when tapped.
6. Remove from pans and serve while hot.

12 rolls

Onion Popcorn

⅓ to ½ cup dry onion soup mix
½ cup melted butter or margarine
3 quarts warm popcorn

Combine onion soup mix and melted butter. Pour over popcorn and toss gently until kernels are coated.

About 3 quarts

Cheese Popcorn

Salt
½ cup grated sharp Cheddar or Parmesan cheese
1 quart hot buttered popcorn

Sprinkle salt and cheese over hot buttered popcorn. Toss lightly.

Cheddar Puffs

¼ cup butter or margarine, softened
2 cups shredded sharp Cheddar cheese (about 8 ounces)
1¼ cups sifted all-purpose flour
¾ teaspoon paprika
¼ teaspoon dry mustard
⅛ teaspoon cayenne pepper

1. Blend butter and cheese until smooth. Mix in a blend of the flour, paprika, dry mustard, and cayenne pepper.
2. Shape dough into rolls about 1¼ inches in diameter. Wrap in waxed paper and chill.
3. Cut into ¼-inch slices. Place about 1 inch apart on lightly greased baking sheets.
4. Bake at 400°F about 8 minutes. Serve hot.

About 4 dozen puffs

Chili and Bean Dip

1 cup pork and beans with tomato sauce
¼ cup mayonnaise
2 tablespoons dry onion soup mix
1 tablespoon chili powder
1 wedge onion
Dairy sour cream or sour cream substitute (page 26)

1. Put all ingredients except sour cream into an electric blender container. Cover and blend.
2. Transfer mixture to a serving dish and stir in sour cream to taste, about ½ cup.
3. Serve **potato chips** and **corn chips** as dippers.

About 2 cups dip

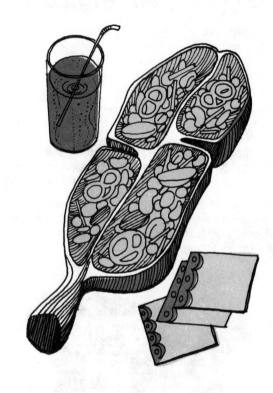

Crunchy Nibblers

2 cups puffed rice cereal
2 cups puffed wheat cereal
1 pound mixed salted nuts
1 can (4 ounces) shoestring potatoes
4 ounces small pretzel rings or sticks
1 cup butter or margarine, melted
¾ teaspoon salt
¾ teaspoon curry powder
¾ teaspoon onion salt
½ teaspoon garlic salt

1. Stir the cereals, nuts, potatoes, and pretzels together in a large shallow baking pan. Blend the remaining ingredients and pour over cereal mixture. Toss lightly with a fork.
2. Heat at 300°F about 30 minutes, stirring several times. Serve warm or cool. Store in tightly covered container in cool dry place.

About 3 quarts

Beverages

Tangy Cider Punch

- ½ cup water
- ¼ cup sugar
- 1 quart apple cider or juice
- ½ cup orange juice
- ¼ cup lemon juice

1. Cook water and sugar together in saucepan, stirring until sugar is dissolved. Boil 5 minutes; cool.
2. Combine cider, orange and lemon juices in a pitcher. Add cooled syrup and serve over ice cubes.
About 5 cups punch

Note: For frozen "slush," put punch in freezer. When crystals start to form, remove from freezer and stir. Stir several times during freezing; serve semi-frozen in cups.

Grapefruit Spritzer

- 1 can (6 ounces) frozen concentrated grapefruit juice, thawed
- 2½ to 3 cups chilled club soda

Pour concentrated grapefruit juice into a pitcher and add chilled club soda slowly; mix well.
About 4 servings

Cocoa Syrup

Use to make chocolate milk or to top a sundae.

- 2 cups sugar
- 1 cup cocoa
- ½ teaspoon salt
- 1 cup cold water
- 1 cup hot water
- 2 teaspoons vanilla extract

Combine the sugar, cocoa, and salt in a saucepan. Stir in cold water to make a paste. Blend in hot water. Simmer 4 to 6 minutes, stirring until thick and smooth. Cool and stir in the extract. Store in a tightly covered container in refrigerator.
About 3 cups

Spicy Iced Tea

- 1 cup water
- 1 cup sugar
- ⅛ teaspoon ground nutmeg
- 6 whole cloves
- 4 whole allspice
- 4 pieces (2 inches each) stick cinnamon
- 3 tablespoons tea or 3 to 5 tea bags

1. Combine all ingredients except tea in a saucepan. Stir over low heat until sugar is dissolved. Cover tightly and simmer 20 minutes. Strain, cool, and chill thoroughly.
2. Bring 2 cups freshly drawn cold water to a full rolling boil in a saucepan. Remove from heat and immediately add the tea; stir. Let tea steep 5 minutes. Stir and drain into a pitcher containing 2 cups cold water. (Remove tea bags, if used, and omit straining.) Blend in the spiced syrup.
3. Pour into ice-filled glasses. Serve with thin slices of **lime** or **lemon**.
About 1 quart

Desserts

Crunchy Honey Granola

2 cups uncooked old-fashioned oats
1 cup toasted wheat germ
½ cup almonds or filberts, chopped
2 tablespoons sesame seed
¼ cup vegetable oil
½ cup honey

1. Put oats, wheat germ, almonds, sesame seed, oil, and honey into a bowl. Stir until well mixed. Turn into a 15×10×1-inch jelly-roll pan and spread evenly.
2. Bake at 275°F about 1 hour, or until toasted as desired, stirring occasionally.
3. Remove from oven and while still hot turn into a bowl. Cool completely. Break into pieces. Store in a tightly covered container.

About 3½ cups granola

Fruit-a-Plenty Pie

1 can (30 ounces) apricot halves
1 package (12 ounces) frozen pineapple chunks, thawed
1 package (8 ounces) cream cheese
2 tablespoons butter or margarine
1 cup Multi-Purpose Baking Mix (page 15)
½ cup sugar
2 tablespoons cornstarch
¼ teaspoon salt
¼ cup lemon juice
¼ teaspoon grated lemon peel
1 pint strawberries, rinsed and halved
1 bunch seedless grapes (about 1½ cups)

1. Drain apricots, reserving syrup. Drain pineapple chunks, reserving syrup. Set all aside.
2. To make crust, cut 3 ounces cream cheese (reserve remaining 5 ounces for use in cream cheese spread) and butter into Baking Mix until mixture resembles coarse crumbs; with hands form into a ball. Pat out dough on a lightly greased 12-inch pizza pan; flute edge. (Crust will be very thin.) Bake in a 425°F oven for about 8 minutes, or until crust is lightly browned; cool.

3. To make glaze, combine in a small saucepan ¼ cup sugar, cornstarch, and salt. Add 1 cup reserved apricot syrup, ½ cup reserved pineapple syrup, and lemon juice. Cook over medium-high heat, stirring constantly, until mixture thickens and begins to boil. Boil and stir 1 minute; cool.
4. To make cream cheese spread, stir remaining cream cheese, 2 tablespoons reserved apricot syrup, remaining ¼ cup of the sugar, and lemon peel until smooth; spread on cooled crust.
5. To assemble pie, arrange fruits in circles on cream cheese spread as follows: Place apricots around outer edge of pie, overlapping slightly. Next, make circle of halved strawberries, then circle of grapes, finally a circle of pineapple chunks. Arrange 3 apricot halves in center of pie. Brush some of glaze over fruits. Cut pie into wedges; serve with remaining glaze mixture.

10 to 12 servings

Oatmeal Cookies

1¼ cups all-purpose flour
½ teaspoon baking soda
1¼ cups uncooked oats
¾ cup margarine
⅔ cup firmly packed brown sugar
¼ cup warm water

1. Blend flour and baking soda, then mix in oats.
2. Cream margarine and brown sugar thoroughly. Add water and mix well. Stir in dry ingredients.
3. Shape dough into small balls, arrange on cookie sheets, and flatten with a fork dipped in water to prevent sticking.
4. Bake at 375°F 6 to 8 minutes, or until golden brown.

About 6 dozen cookies

Lemon Bellringer Cake

1 package (18½ or 19 ounces) lemon cake mix
1 package (3 ounces) lemon-flavored gelatin
¾ cup water
¾ cup vegetable oil
4 eggs
1 teaspoon vanilla extract
Topping (see recipe)

1. Combine all ingredients except topping in large bowl of electric mixer. Beat 30 seconds; stop mixer and scrape beater and bowl. Beat 4 minutes longer at medium speed.
2. Pour batter into a greased and floured 13×9×2-inch pan.
3. Bake at 350°F about 35 minutes, or until cake is golden and springs back when lightly touched.
4. Remove cake from oven. While still hot, prick holes ¾ of the way through cake with fork. Spread topping evenly over top.

One 13×9-inch cake

Topping: Mix 1 cup confectioners' sugar with ¼ cup lemon juice until evenly combined.

Frosted Cocoa Cupcakes

1¼ cups sifted all-purpose flour
½ cup cocoa, sifted
½ teaspoon baking powder
½ teaspoon baking soda
Milk (about ½ cup)
1½ teaspoons cider vinegar
½ cup butter
1½ teaspoons vanilla extract
1 cup sugar
1 egg
½ cup hot water

Chocolate-Cola Frosting:
1 package chocolate fudge frosting mix
Cola beverage

1. Sift the flour, cocoa, baking powder, and baking soda together and blend thoroughly; set aside.
2. Add enough milk to vinegar to measure ½ cup liquid; set aside.
3. Cream the butter with vanilla extract. Gradually add sugar, creaming until fluffy. Add egg and beat thoroughly.

4. Beating only until smooth after each addition, alternately add dry ingredients in fourths and a mixture of milk and hot water in thirds to creamed mixture. Spoon mixture into 2½-inch muffin-pan wells lined with paper baking cups or greased (bottoms only), filling each one-half to two-thirds full.
5. Bake at 375°F about 20 minutes, or until cakes test done.
6. Remove from pans and cool. Frost with Chocolate-Cola Frosting.
7. For frosting, prepare frosting mix as directed on package, substituting cola beverage for the liquid. Beat until of spreading consistency.

About 16 cupcakes

Frosted Peanut Butter Cupcakes

2 cups sifted cake flour
2½ teaspoons baking powder
½ teaspoon salt
⅓ cup shortening
1 teaspoon vanilla extract
1 cup lightly packed brown sugar
½ cup peanut butter
2 eggs
½ cup lightly packed brown sugar
¾ cup milk

Creamy Peanut Butter Frosting:
6 tablespoons butter
1½ tablespoons peanut butter
¾ teaspoon vanilla extract
2½ cups confectioners' sugar
1 egg yolk
Milk (about 1½ tablespoons)

1. For cupcakes, blend flour, baking powder, and salt; set aside.
2. Cream shortening and vanilla extract; gradually

add the 1 cup brown sugar, creaming well. Beat in the peanut butter until thoroughly blended.

3. Beat eggs with remaining ½ cup brown sugar until thick. Add to creamed mixture and beat well.

4. Beating only until smooth after each addition, alternately add dry ingredients in fourths and milk in thirds to creamed mixture. Line 2½-inch muffin-pan wells with paper baking cups or grease (bottoms only). Fill each well about one-half full with batter.

5. Bake at 350°F 25 to 30 minutes, or until cakes test done.

6. Remove from pans and cool.

7. For frosting, cream butter with peanut butter and vanilla extract.

8. Gradually add the confectioners' sugar, beating well after each addition. Beat in egg yolk.

9. Beat in enough of the milk until frosting is of spreading consistency. Frost cupcakes.

About 2 dozen cupcakes

Blueberry Pie (60-Second Version)

    2 cups fresh blueberries, washed and drained, or frozen dry-pack blueberries
    1 can (21 ounces) blueberry pie filling
    1 baked 10-inch pie shell
      Whipped cream

Fold fresh blueberries into blueberry pie filling, and turn mixture into pie shell. Refrigerate. Garnish with whipped cream at serving time.

One 10-inch pie

Bird's Nest Pudding

    2 cups sugar
    1 cup water
    ¼ teaspoon red food coloring
    6 medium apples, washed, cored, and pared (keep whole)
    3 eggs
    ¼ cup sugar
    2 teaspoons vanilla extract
    2 cups cream, scalded

1. Add the 2 cups sugar to the water in a large saucepan; bring to boiling, stirring until sugar is dissolved. Mix in the food coloring.

2. Add as many apples as will fit uncrowded in the saucepan; cover and cook slowly until apples are just tender, about 7 minutes, turning carefully several times to obtain an even color. With a slotted spoon, transfer apples to a 1½-quart baking dish.

3. Combine eggs, the ¼ cup sugar, and vanilla extract in a bowl; beat just until blended. Gradually add the hot cream, stirring until sugar is dissolved. Strain mixture through a fine sieve over apples in the baking dish. Set dish in a larger pan on oven rack; pour boiling water into pan to a depth of at least 1 inch.

4. Bake at 325°F 50 to 60 minutes.

6 servings

Peanut-Pudding Squares

    1 package (3¾ ounces) butterscotch pudding and pie filling
    2 cups milk
    ¼ cup creamy peanut butter
    3 tablespoons soft butter or margarine
    1¼ cups coarse graham-cracker crumbs

1. Prepare pudding mix with the milk as directed on package; set aside.

2. Combine peanut butter and butter with pudding and mix well.

3. Spread ¾ cup crumbs in greased 8-inch square pan. Cover with 1 cup cooled pudding. Alternate layers of crumb mixture and cooled pudding, ending with crumb mixture. Chill about 4 hours.

6 servings

Frozen Lemon Velvet

    1 can (13 ounces) evaporated milk
    2½ cups graham cracker crumbs
    ⅔ cup margarine, melted
    2 packages (8 ounces each) cream cheese,
        softened
    1 cup sugar
    2 tablespoons milk
    2 tablespoons grated lemon peel
    1 cup chopped walnuts

1. Pour evaporated milk into a refrigerator tray, and set in freezer until ice crystals form around edges.
2. Combine cracker crumbs and margarine. Turn into a 13×9-inch pan and press into an even layer.
3. Put cream cheese, sugar, milk, and lemon peel into a bowl; mix until smooth.
4. Turn icy cold evaporated milk into a chilled bowl and beat with a chilled beater until stiff peaks are formed. Fold whipped evaporated milk and nuts into cheese mixture; turn onto layer in pan and spread evenly. Freeze.
5. To serve, cut into squares and garnish with lemon slices and **graham cracker crumbs**.

16 to 20 servings

Chocolate Peanut Treats

    2 cups sugar
    ¼ cup unsweetened cocoa
    ½ cup milk
    1 tablespoon light corn syrup
    ½ cup butter or margarine
    2 cups quick-cooking oats
    ¼ cup peanut butter

1. In a heavy saucepan, combine sugar and cocoa; stir in milk and corn syrup.
2. Add butter. Bring to boiling; boil vigorously 3 minutes.
3. Stir in rolled oats and peanut butter. Return to boil.
4. Remove from heat; stir until slightly thickened. Immediately drop by teaspoonfuls onto waxed paper. Cool.

About 4 dozen

Hermits

    1 cup dark seedless raisins
    2½ cups sifted all-purpose flour
    ¾ teaspoon baking soda
    ½ teaspoon salt
    1 teaspoon ground cinnamon
    ½ teaspoon ground nutmeg
    ⅛ teaspoon ground cloves
    ¾ cup butter
    1½ cups firmly packed brown sugar
    3 eggs
    1 cup walnuts, chopped

1. Pour 2 cups boiling water over raisins in a saucepan and bring to boiling; pour off water and drain raisins on absorbent paper. Coarsely chop raisins and set aside.
2. Sift flour, baking soda, salt, and spices together and blend thoroughly; set aside.
3. Cream butter; add brown sugar gradually, beating until fluffy. Add eggs, one at a time, beating thoroughly after each addition.
4. Add dry ingredients in fourths, mixing until blended after each addition. Stir in raisins and walnuts.
5. Drop by teaspoonfuls 2 inches apart onto lightly greased cookie sheets.
6. Bake at 400°F about 7 minutes.

About 8 dozen cookies

MENU PLANS FOR TWO WEEKS

Here are two-weeks' worth of menus, planned for a family with two adults and two teenagers, or three smaller children.

These menus have been put into actual practice, and have won one family's seal of approval. But each family has its own preferences, and individuals within families will have their own personal tastes. If you plan to try these meals, it would be a good idea to check them over. Some selections may need to be tailored for your family, and others can be dropped to accommodate special bargains at the store.

The shopping list that accompanies each week's menus includes perishables and a few staple items. Nobody buys all staples every week. Such things as tea, coffee, flour, and sugar need replacement from time to time. During that weekly cleanout and inventory, add those items to your shopping list.

A decorated warrior from the budget battle may find many points at which these menus could be made more economical; we all know a few people who use parings, peelings, and such. While not that frugal, our total at the cash register fell well within the U.S.D.A.'s guideline for low-cost meals. Our menus meet the requirements for nutrition. And our tasters scored them high on appeal . . . a good bargain, all around!

MENUS FOR A FAMILY OF FOUR WEEK 1

 Sunday

Breakfast
Sliced Oranges
Baked Eggs
Oatmeal Muffins (page 21) and Jelly
Coffee   Milk

Dinner
Roast Turkey with Cooked Giblets and Herbed Stuffing (page 58)
Turkey Roasting Pan Gravy (page 59)
Mashed Potatoes
Lima Beans
Molded Fruit Salad
Family Cake with Broiled Topping (page 16)
Tea   Milk

Snack
Tomato Soup
Fruit and Cheese Tray
Crackers   Milk

Monday

Breakfast
Orange Juice
Cooked Cereal
Cinnamon Toast
Coffee   Milk

Lunch
Turkey Sandwich (leftover turkey)
Molded Fruit Salad (leftover)
Milk

Dinner
Sloppy Joes from Hamburger Mix (page 19)
Tossed Green Salad with French Dressing (page 21)
Family Cake with Ice Milk
Coffee   Milk

Tuesday

Breakfast
Banana Slices in Orange Juice
French Toast with Homemade Syrup
Coffee   Milk

Lunch
Grilled Cheese Sandwiches
Carrot Sticks
Leftover Family Cake
Milk

Dinner
Hearty Poultry Pie (page 38)
Lettuce Wedge with Chiffonade Dressing (page 22)
Fresh Fruit
Tea   Milk

Wednesday

Breakfast
Tomato Juice
Scrambled Eggs   Toast
Coffee   Milk

Lunch
Turkey Salad
Fresh Fruit   Toast
Milk

Dinner
Fish Fillets (page 54) with Lemon Wedge
Parsley-Buttered Potatoes
Spinach Salad
Ice Milk with Cocoa Syrup (page 78)
Coffee   Milk

Thursday

Breakfast
Grape Juice
Cereal with Banana Topping
Toast
Coffee   Milk

Lunch
Peanut Butter Sandwiches
Carrot Sticks
Cookies   Milk

Dinner
Turkey Soup (page 39)
Baking Powder Biscuits (page 16)
Jelly
Pear Salad with Shredded Cheddar Cheese
Nutty Chocolate Pudding (page 18)
Tea   Milk

Friday

Breakfast
Grape Juice
Oatmeal with Brown Sugar
Toast
Coffee   Milk

Lunch
Lunchmeat Open-Faced Sandwich
Deviled Eggs
Fresh Fruit   Milk

Dinner
Savory Swiss Steak Strips (page 50)
French Fried Potatoes
Tart Cabbage Slaw (page 74)
Ice Milk Shakes

Saturday

Breakfast
Grapefruit Halves or Melon Wedges
Pancakes (page 16)
Homemade Syrup
Coffee   Milk

Lunch
Frankfurter-Chicken Cream Soup (page 42)
Oatmeal Muffins (page 21)   Honey
Milk

Dinner
Penny-wise Pizza (page 29)
Tossed Green Salad with Italian Dressing
(page 24)
Fruit Bowl
Tea   Milk

SHOPPING LIST FOR FAMILY MENUS WEEK 1

Bakery

1 loaf white bread
3 loaves whole wheat
1 loaf day-old bread for stuffing

Canned Foods

Grape juice (fortified)
Tomato juice
Tomato sauce
Tomato soup

Dairy Foods and Eggs

5 gallons milk
1 pound process American cheese
1 pound margarine
1 pound Cheddar cheese
2 dozen eggs

Frozen Foods

Orange juice
½ gallon ice milk
French fried potatoes, large poly-bag
Lima beans, large poly-bag

Meat, Poultry, and Fish

Young Tom turkey, 15 pounds or more
1 pound lunchmeat
1½ pounds fish fillets
3 pounds round steak
4 pounds ground beef

Packaged Foods

Fruit-flavored gelatin
Packaged cereal, 2 or 3
Oats
Cookies

Produce

Fruits
Bananas
Oranges
Select two or three other fruits in
season
Vegetables
Cabbage
Carrots
Celery
Lettuce
Onions
Parsley
Potatoes
Spinach

Miscellaneous

Ketchup, 24 ounces or more

MENUS FOR A FAMILY OF FOUR WEEK 2

Sunday

Breakfast
> Citrus Fruit Cup
> Waffles (page 17)   Homemade Syrup
> Coffee   Milk

Dinner
> Oven-Baked Smoked Pork Shoulder
> Baked Sweet or White Potatoes
> Peas
> Lettuce Wedge with Lorenzo Dressing
>   (page 22)
> Chocolate Cake (page 17)
> Tea   Coffee   Milk

Snack
> Popcorn
> Fruit Bowl
> Spicy Iced Tea (page 78)

Monday

Breakfast
> Orange Juice
> Eggs Sunnyside
> Wheat Toast
> Coffee   Milk

Lunch
> Peanut Butter Sandwiches
> Carrot Sticks
> Bananas
> Milk

Dinner
> Cheese-Onion Pie (page 71)
> Molded Fruit Salad in Lettuce Cups
> Chocolate Cake with Ice Milk
> Tea   Milk

Tuesday

Breakfast
> Stewed Prunes in Orange Juice
> Cereal
> Cinnamon Toast
> Coffee   Milk

Lunch
> Creamed Hard-Cooked Eggs on Toast
> Fruit Mold
> Cake or Cookies   Milk

Dinner
> Casserole of Leftover Smoked Pork and
>   Green Beans
> Coleslaw
> Fruit Crisp (page 18)
> Coffee   Milk

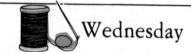

Wednesday

Breakfast
> Tomato Juice
> French Toast   Homemade Syrup
> Coffee   Milk

Lunch
> Franks in Buns
> Celery Strips
> Fresh Fruit   Milk

Dinner
> Pot Roast Piquante (page 47)
> Pan Gravy
> Boiled Potatoes
> Tossed Green Salad with Curried French
>   Dressing (page 22)
> Brownies
> Tea   Milk

Thursday

Breakfast
> Orange Slices
> Scrambled Eggs (page 68)   Toast
> Coffee   Milk

Lunch
- Bean Soup with Frank Chunks
- Carrot Sticks
- Chocolate Peanut Treats (page 82)
- Milk

Dinner
- Mackerel Patties (page 57)
- Canned Shoestring Potatoes
- Cornbread
- Broccoli
- Ice Milk with Fruit Topping
- Coffee   Milk

Friday

Breakfast
- Grape Juice
- Pancakes   Homemade Syrup
- Coffee   Milk

Lunch
- Creamed Tuna on Reheated Cornbread
- Celery Sticks
- Bananas   Milk

Dinner
- Pot Roast Cubes and Vegetables in Gravy
  on Noodles
- Spinach Salad
- Broiled Grapefruit Halves
- Tea   Milk

Saturday

Breakfast
- Cranberry or Grape Juice
- Omelets   Toast
- Coffee   Milk

Lunch
- Chicken Soup
- Lunchmeat Sandwiches
- Fresh Fruit   Milk

Dinner
- Spaghetti and Hamburger Mix (page 19)
- Italian Dressing on Torn Greens
- Bread Sticks
- Sherbet
- Coffee   Milk

SHOPPING LIST
FOR FAMILY MENUS
WEEK 2

 Bakery

- Bread sticks
- Frankfurter buns
- 1 loaf enriched white bread
- 3 loaves whole wheat bread

 Dairy Foods and Eggs

- 1 pound Cheddar cheese
- 2 dozen eggs
- 1 pound margarine
- 5 gallons milk

 Canned Foods

- Soups
  - Bean
  - Chicken
- Juices
  - Cranberry
  - Grape
  - Tomato
- Vegetables
  - Green beans
  - Peas
  - Shoestring potatoes
- Other
  - Mackerel
  - Tuna (chunk style)

 Frozen Foods

- Broccoli
- ½ gallon ice milk
- Orange juice
- Sherbet

Meat, Poultry, and Fish

4 pounds beef blade pot roast
1 pound franks
1 pound lunchmeat
3 pounds smoked pork shoulder roll

 ## Packaged Foods

Cocoa
Cookies
Fruit-flavored gelatin
Noodles
Packaged cereal, 2 or 3
Peanut butter
Spaghetti

 ## Produce

Fruits
    Bananas
    Grapefruit
    Oranges
    Prunes
    Select two or three other fruits in
        season
Vegetables
    Cabbage
    Carrots
    Celery
    Green pepper
    Lettuce
    Onions
    Spinach
    Potatoes

HOW LONG WILL IT KEEP?

REFRIGERATOR STORAGE

Just as "a penny saved is a penny earned," a bonus meal in the refrigerator is like money in the bank. How you wrap and how long you store will have a lot to do with how palatable those leftovers are, second time around.

WRAPPINGS

Original containers work best for many foods. Milk and other dairy products keep best in their own cartons. Eggs are better left in the carton, too, despite those handy racks in the refrigerator door. Cooked food and liquids can be kept in plastic refrigerator containers with tight fitting lids. Plastic bags are fine for fresh produce and baked goods that need refrigerating.

Opened canned foods can be refrigerated in the original can with a tight cover. Acid foods and juices, such as tomato juice, fruits, and tomatoes, may pick up a "tinny" flavor if left in the can, so you may prefer to transfer them to plastic containers.

COOL IT

Refrigerate leftover foods right after eating; there is no advantage in letting things cool to room temperature first. It's at room temperature that food poisoning microorganisms work best; in four hours at 70°F they can do serious damage. So cool it in a hurry.

REFRIGERATOR STORAGE LIMITS

Food	Storage limit (36° to 40°F)
BREADS	Don't refrigerate
DAIRY FOODS	
Fresh milk and cream	4 days
Evaporated and sweetened condensed milk (opened)	7 days
Cheese	
cream and cottage	10 days
Cheddar, Swiss, and other hard cheese	3 months
spreads	3 weeks
EGGS	1 to 2 weeks
FISH	
Fresh fish	2 days
Smoked fish	6 to 8 weeks
FRUITS	
Fresh	about 7 days (varies)
Canned (opened)	5 days
Juices, canned (opened)	5 days
MEAT	
Cooked meat, leftover	4 to 5 days
Corned beef	7 days

Food	*Storage limit (36° to 40°F)*
Fresh meat (beef, lamb, pork, veal)	
ground	1 to 2 days
roasts	4 days
steaks and chops	2 days
Smoked meat	
bacon, franks	5 days
ham (whole or half)	7 days
ham slices	4 days
Sausage	
dry and semi-dry, un-sliced	1 month
dry and semi-dry (sliced, opened)	2 weeks
frankfurters	5 days
fresh pork	7 days
luncheon meats (sliced)	7 days

POULTRY

Chicken, uncooked, whole or cut up	2 days
Cooked poultry, leftover	3 days
Turkey, thawed whole	2 days

VEGETABLES

Fresh	about 7 days (varies)
Cooked and canned (opened)	3 days

FREEZER STORAGE

The temperature inside the home freezer should be kept at around zero degrees. You'll know if it goes higher because the ice cream will start to get mushy.

Foods that have been kept frozen won't cause food poisoning because the low temperature puts the microorganisms out of business, but there's another villain to avoid—freezer burn. This condition develops when air creeps into the package. The food dries out, and in the case of meat especially, takes on an unappealing brown cast.

Money spent on freezer wrap is well invested. Freezer paper, foil, and special freezer plastic bags all do the job. Air must be pressed out of packages, and the seal must be tight so none can get back in.

DON'T FREEZE AND THEN FORGET

An inventory is the best way to assure a steady turnover of food from the freezer. Date food as it goes into the freezer (use a marker on the masking tape that seals the package); then remember to use it within the recommended storage time. A list, perhaps taped to the freezer door, is a good way to remember what's on hand. Make a note as you remove food, just as you do when it goes in.

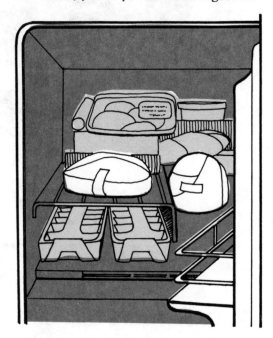

FREEZER STORAGE LIMITS

Food	*Storage limit (around 0°F)*
BAKED AND COOKED FOODS	
Breads (baked)	3 months
Breads (unbaked dough)	1 month
Cakes (frosted)	2 months
Cakes (unfrosted)	3 months
Cookies (baked or dough)	9 months
Pies (baked)	3 months
Pies (unbaked)	4 months
Pie shells	2 months
Sandwiches	1 month
Leftover cooked foods, casseroles, etc.	1 month
Prepared main dishes, soups, stews	3 months
DAIRY PRODUCTS	
Creamery butter	5 months
Cottage cheese (not creamed)	6 months
Natural cheese (Cheddar, Swiss, mozzarella, etc.) small packages, 1 pound or less	3 months

Cream (half-and-half)	4 months	Ground meats	3 months
Cream, whipped	1 month	Smoked ham, franks, bacon	1 month
Ice cream	2 months	Variety meats	4 months
Milk (homogenized)	1 month	Leftover cooked meat	3 months

EGGS

Eggs (whole or yolks, 1 teaspoon salt or 1 tablespoon sugar to each cup of eggs)   12 months

Egg whites   9 months

Cooked meat and vegetable combinations   3 months

Poultry
  Chicken (cut up)   6 months
  Chicken and turkey (whole)   8 months
  Poultry giblets   3 months

MEAT, POULTRY, AND FISH

Meat

Beef roasts	12 months
Beef steaks	8 months
Lamb roasts	9 months
Lamb chops	4 months
Pork roasts	6 months
Pork chops	4 months

Fish
  Fatty fish   3 months
  Lean fish   4 months
  Salmon   6 months

VEGETABLES AND FRUIT   12 months

PROPER FREEZER WRAP-UP

Drug Store Wrap   Wrapping in Freezer Bag

INDEX

ABC of leftovers, 35

Bacon
ABC of leftovers, 35
fat, 35
omelet, 69
storage limits
freezer, 91
refrigerator, 90
Baking
mix, multi-purpose, 15
powder, substitutes for, 25
Beef
bone shapes indicate cooking
methods, 47
broth, substitutes for, 25
-curry skillet bake, 40
freezer storage limits, 91
ground
balls in tomato sauce, porcu-
pine, 47
-eggplant casserole, 48
hamburger mix, 19
meat loaf à la Wellington, 48
-noodle scallop, 65
patchwork casserole, 50
tagliarini, 64
twosome meat loaf, 34
heart, glazed stuffed, 53
meat-cottage cheese mold, 38
pot roast piquante, 47
ragout of, Hunstman, 45
refrigerator storage limits, 89–90
sauerbraten, 27
sirloin tip roast with Parmesan
barbecue baste, 49
spiced short ribs with cabbage, 45
stroganoff, economy class, 30
Swiss steak
in vegetable sauce, 49
strips, savory, 50
versatile meat-vegetable casserole, 48
with onion (stifado), 43
Beverages
cocoa
mix, cheaper to do-it-yourself,
14, 24
syrup, 78
fruit drinks, cheaper to do-it-
yourself, 14
grapefruit spritzer, 78
spicy iced tea, 78
tangy cider punch, 78
Borsch, 41
Bread(s)
ABC of leftovers, 35

biscuits
baking powder, 16
oatmeal, 21
brioche, 28
cheaper to do-it-yourself
muffins, 13
variations, 13
commercially baked loaves,
cheaper to buy in the convenience forms, 14
crumbs, dry, substitutes for, 25
freezer storage limits, 90
muffins
cheaper to do-it-yourself, 13
oatmeal, 21
oatmeal
biscuits, 21
muffins, 21
quick applesauce, 21
refrigerator storage limits, 89
Brioche, 28
Budgeting for one or two
batching it, 31
planning for the couple, 31
shopping list, 33
week's menus, 32
Budget-saving recipes
egg and cheese dishes, 68–71
fish, 54–57
fruits and vegetables, 73–75
meat, 47–53
pasta and other cereal dishes,
64–66
poultry, 58–62
soups and stews, 41–45
treats
beverages, 78
desserts, 79–82
snacks, 76–77
Butter
creamery, freezer storage
limits, 90
substitutes for, 25

Cakes, see Desserts
Casserole(s)
cheeseroni, 64
freezer storage limits, 90
green bean-pork chop, 51
ground beef-eggplant, 48
mackerel, 57
patchwork, 50
penny-wise chicken, 59
pork, macaroni, and vegetable, 40
spaghetti, 66
sweet potato-rice, 66
tuna, 55
and noodle, Florentine, 56
broccoli, and macaroni, 56
choose-a-partner, 56
green beans, and rice, 56
versatile meat-vegetable, 48

Cereal(s)
ABC of leftovers, 35
breakfast, cheaper to do-it-
yourself, 13
chocolate farina, substitute for,
25
Cheese
ABC of leftovers, 35
Cheddar
freezer storage limits, 90
puffs, 77
refrigerator storage limits, 89
substitute for, 25
cottage
freezer storage limits (not
creamed), 90
refrigerator storage limits, 89
rolls, 76
cream, refrigerator storage limits,
89
freezer storage limits, 90
hard, refrigerator storage limits,
89
measuring for recipes, 68
natural, 67, 90
-onion pie, 71
process, 68
puff, parsleyed, 71
refrigerator storage limits, 89
sauce on toast, mushroom, 70
shirred eggs with sausage and, 69
soufflé, 70
spreads, refrigerator storage limits, 89
strata, 70
Swiss
and tuna pie, 70
refrigerator storage limits, 89
substitute for, 25
Welsh rabbit in chafing dish, 71
Chicken
ABC of leftovers, 36
baked with seasoned coating mix,
16
casa, 61
casserole
penny-wise, 59
versatile meat-vegetable, 48
cheaper to do-it-yourself
seasoned coating mix, 14
whole, 13
denim dumpling dinner, 62
freezer storage limits
cut-up, 91
whole, 91
fried, à la southern belle, 61
hearty poultry pie, 38
how to cut up a whole broiler-
fryer, 60
liver(s)
omelet, 69
pâté exceptionale, 29

sautéed, 61
superb, 60
meat-cottage cheese mold, 38
paprika, 62
refrigerator storage limits
cooked, 90
uncooked, 90
specialty, ham 'n', 66
substitutes for
broth, 25
cooked, 25
Chili
chowder, tuna-, 55
con carne, quick, 20
sauce, substitute for, 26
Chocolate, substitutes for
pieces, semisweet for melting
only, 26
unsweetened, 26
Chowder
Dutch style, 41
tuna-chili, 55
Cocoa
mix, cheaper to do-it-yourself,
14, 24
syrup, 78
Corned beef
"boiled" dinner, 44
refrigerator storage limits, 89
Cornstarch, substitute for, 26
Cream
substitutes for
sour, 26
whipped, 26
whipping, 26
whipped, freezer storage limits,
91

Daily Food Guide, 11
Dessert(s)
cakes
chocolate, 17
freezer storage limits, 90
lemon, 17
lemon bellringer, 80
with broiled topping, family, 16
cheaper to buy in the convenience forms
cake mixes, 14
flavored gelatin, 14
ice cream, 14
packaged pudding mix, 14
chocolate peanut treats, 82
cookies
freezer storage limits, 90
hermits, 82
oatmeal, 79
crunchy honey granola, 79
cupcakes
frosted cocoa, 80
frosted peanut butter, 80
frozen lemon velvet, 82

fruit cobbler, 18
fruit crisp, 18
peanut-pudding squares, 81
pie(s)
blueberry (60-second version),
81
crust mix, 18
freezer storage limits, 90
fruit-a-plenty, 79
pastry for 1-crust, 19
pastry for 2-crust, 19
puddings
bird's nest, 81
nutty chocolate, 18

Dip, chili and bean, 77
Dumpling(s)
dinner, denim, 62
fluffy, 21
potato (Kartoffelklösse), 28

Egg(s)
ABC of leftovers, 36
buying, 67
color, 67
Florentine à l'orange, 69
freezer storage limits
white, 91
whole or yolks, 91
grades, 67
omelet
bacon, 69
chicken liver, 69
citrus, 69
French, 68
poached, 68
scrambled, 68
deluxe, 68
in salami cups, 34
with sausage and cheese, shirred,
69

Fillings, sandwich, cheaper to do-
it-yourself, 13
Fish
ABC of leftovers, 36
canned, cheaper to buy in the
convenience forms, 14
fillet dinner, planked, 54
fillets, 54
freezer storage limits
fatty, 91
lean, 91
mackerel
and macaroni with green beans,
57
casserole, 57
patties, 57
poached in court bouillon, 54
refrigerator storage limits
fresh, 89
smoked, 89

salmon, freezer storage limits, 91
smelts, fried, 54
stick special, 56
tuna
casseroles, 55–56
-chili chowder, 55
pie, blushing, 57
pie, Swiss and, 70
supreme, skillet, 55
Flour, substitutes for
cake, 26
thickening, 26
Frankfurter(s)
-chicken cream soup, 42
storage limits
freezer, 91
refrigerator, 90
Freezer storage
don't freeze and then forget, 90
limits, 90
proper freezer wrap-up, 91
Frosting
chocolate-cola, 80
creamy peanut butter, 80
Fruit(s)
ABC of leftovers, 36
blueberry pie (60-second version), 81
canned, 72
cheaper to buy in the convenience forms
bottled lemon juice, 14
commercially canned and frozen, 14
frozen orange juice, 14
drinks, cheaper to do-it-yourself,
14
freezer storage limits, 91
fresh produce, 72
frozen, 72
honey French dressing for, 23
refrigerator storage limits
canned (opened), 89
fresh, 89
juices, canned (opened), 89

Garlic, substitutes for, 26
Giblets
and broth, cooked, 59
freezer storage limits, 91
roast turkey with cooked, 58
Goulash, szekely, 43
Gourmet dining on a budget, 27–30
Gravy
ABC of leftovers, 36
gingersnap, 28
turkey roasting pan, 59

Half-and-half
freezer storage limits, 91
substitute for, 26

Ham
  balls in sour cream sauce, 37
  -bean soup, 37
  freezer storage limits, 91
  loaf, glazed, 36
  meat-cottage cheese mold, 38
  'n' chicken specialty, 66
  'n' taters, 37
  refrigerator storage limits
    slices, 90
    whole or half, 90
Hamburger
  meat 'n' biscuit bake, 20
  meaty roll-ups, 20
  mix, 19
  quick chili con carne, 20
  sauce
    cheaper to do-it-yourself, 14
    spaghetti, 19
  sauced pinwheels, 20
  sloppy joes, 19
  stuffed cabbage leaves, 19
Heart, glazed stuffed beef, 53
Herb(s)
  bouquet, 55
  cheaper to buy in the conve-
    nience forms
    dried, 14
    freeze-dried, 14
    frozen, 14
  substitutes for, 26
Homemade mixes
  basic oats mix, 20
  French dressing mix, 21
  hamburger mix, 19
  Italian dressing mix, 24
  multi-purpose baking mix, 15
  pie crust mix, 18
Honey, substitute for, 26

Ice cream
  cheaper to buy in the conve-
    nience forms, 14
  freezer storage limits, 91

Jelly, ABC of leftovers, 36

Kartoffelklösse (potato dumplings),
    28
Kidneys in rice ring, herbed lamb,
    52

Lamb
  bone shapes indicate cooking
    methods, 47
  freezer storage limits
    chops, 91
    cooked meat and vegetable
      combinations, 91
    leftover cooked meat, 91
    roast, 91
  kidneys in rice ring, herbed, 52

refrigerator storage limits
    cooked, 89
    fresh, 90
  shanks, barbecued, 52
  stew, oven, 44
  superb, spicy, 51
  versatile meat-vegetable casse-
    role, 48
Lasagne, lowcost, 30
Leftovers
  ABC of, 35
  freezer storage limits, 90
  recipes, 36–40
  thrifty use of, 9
Liver(s)
  à la Madame Begue, 52
  chicken
    omelet, 69
    sautéed, 61
    superb, 60
  on skewers, 53
Lunchmeat
  cheaper to do-it-yourself, 13
  refrigerator storage limits, 90

Macaroni, see Pasta
Mackerel
  and macaroni with green beans,
    57
  casserole, 57
  patties, 57
Make or buy
  cheaper to buy in the conve-
    nience forms, 14
  cheaper to do-it-yourself, 13
Marshmallows, substitute for, 26
Meat(s)
  ABC of leftovers, 36
  bone shape is a guide to tender-
    ness, 47
  bone shapes indicate cooking
    methods, 47
  cottage cheese mold, 38
  freezer storage limits, 91
  grading and inspection, 46
  learn to figure savings per pound,
    46
  loaf
    à la Wellington, 48
    twosome, 34
  refrigerator storage limits, 89–90
  -vegetable casserole, versatile, 48
Menus (week's)
  for a family of 4
    week 1, 83
    week 2, 86
  for a twosome or live-aloner, 32
  shopping lists, 33, 85, 87
Milk
  freezer storage limits, 91
  refrigerator storage limits
    evaporated, 89

fresh, 89
  sweetened condensed, 89
  substitutes for
    sour, 26
    whole, 26
Mold, meat-cottage cheese, 38
Mushroom
  bake, turkey, 40
  cheese sauce on toast, 70
Mustard
  prepared, substitutes for, 26
  sauce, 51

Noodles, see Pasta
Nutrition labeling and other label-
    ing information, 10
Nuts, cheaper to do-it-yourself, 14

Oil, for frying, substitutes for, 26
Omelet
  bacon, 69
  chicken liver, 69
  citrus, 69
  French, 68
Oxtail stew, German style, 44

Pancakes, 16
Parmesan barbecue baste, 49
Pasta
  casseroles
    cheeseroni, 64
    choose-a-partner tuna, 56
    pork, macaroni, and vegetable,
      40
    spaghetti, 66
    tuna and noodle, Florentine, 56
    tuna, broccoli, and macaroni, 56
  freezer storage limits, 90
  garlic-buttered fusilli, 66
  German noodle ring, 64
  ground beef-noodle scallop, 65
  ham 'n' chicken specialty, 66
  products, 63
  shapes, some, 63
  tagliarini, 64
  turkey-tomato mac, 65
Pastitsio, budget style, 28
Peanut butter
  frosting, creamy, 80
  soup, 43
Peppers, stuffed, 74
Pickle juice, ABC of leftovers, 36
Pies, see Desserts
Pizza, penny-wise, 29
Plan to save—to save, plan
  best-laid plans, 10
  can she bake a cherry pie? 12
  cook's other resources—time and
    energy, 12
  daily food guide, 11
  how does your plan stack up? 10

moment of decision—which
    brand?- 10
nutrition, 9
nutrition labeling and other label
    information, 10
once-a-week inventory and stock
    taking, 10
protection against impulse buy-
    ing, 9
thrifty use of leftovers, 9
Polenta with meat sauce, 30
Popcorn
    cheaper to do-it-yourself, 14
    cheese, 77
    onion, 77
Pork
    ABC of leftovers, 36
    bacon, 35
    bacon fat, 35
    bone shapes indicate cooking
        methods, 47
    chop casserole, green bean-, 51
    freezer storage limits
        chops, 91
        cooked meat and vegetable
            combinations, 91
        leftover cooked meat, 91
        roasts, 91
    macaroni and vegetable casserole,
        40
    Pennsylvania Dutch style, roast,
        50
    refrigerator storage limits
        cooked, 89
        fresh, 90
    smoked shoulder roll with mus-
        tard sauce, 51
Poultry, see specific kinds
Puddings, see Desserts

Refrigerator storage
    cool it, 89
    limits, 89
    wrappings, 89
Rice
    ABC of leftovers, 36
    brown, 63
    casserole, sweet potato-, 66
    fried, 65
    pilaf, 64
    precooked, 63
    regular milled, 63
    ring
        herbed lamb kidneys in, 52
        parsley, 52
    wild, 63

Salad(s)
    Greek, 24
    Italian potato, 74
    tart cabbage slaw, 74
Salad dressing(s)

anchovy, 24
blue cheese, 24
cheaper to do-it-yourself, 14
French
    blue cheese, 22
    chiffonade, 22
    curried, 22
    garlic, 22
    honey, for fruit, 23
    Lorenzo, 22
    onion, 24
    tomato, 23
    vinaigrette, 23
    with herbs, 23
Italian, 24
Salami cups, scrambled eggs in, 34
Sandwich(es)
    fillings, cheaper to do-it-yourself,
        13
    freezer storage limits, 90
    turkey fondue, 38
Sauce(s)
    meat, 30
    mushroom cheese, on toast, 70
    spaghetti, 19
    substitutes for
        chili, 26
        tomato, 26
Sauerbraten, 27
Sausage
    ABC of leftovers, 36
    and cheese, shirred eggs with, 69
    refrigerator storage limits
        dry and semi-dry, sliced,
            opened, 90
        dry and semi-dry, unsliced, 90
Seasoned coating mix
    cheaper to do-it-yourself, 14
    chicken baked with, 16
Sloppy joes, 19
Smelts, fried, 54
Snacks
    cheaper to buy in the conve-
        nience forms
        flavored gelatin, 14
        packaged pudding mix, 14
    Cheddar puffs, 77
    chili and bean dip, 77
    cottage cheese rolls, 76
    crunchy nibblers, 77
    fruit drinks, cheaper to do-it-
        yourself, 14
    popcorn
        cheaper to do-it-yourself, 14
        cheese, 77
        onion, 77
Soufflé
    cheese, 70
    turkey, 38
Soups and stews
    ABC of leftovers, 36
    beef, 42

beef with onions (stifado), 43
"boiled" dinner, 44
Borsch, 41
cabbage, 42
Dutch-style chowder, 41
frankfurter-chicken cream, 42
freezer storage limits, 90
German style, oxtail, 44
ham-bean, 37
oven lamb, 44
peanut butter, 43
plantation, 42
ragout of beef Hunstman, 45
spiced short ribs with cabbage, 45
szekely goulash, 43
turkey, 39
Spaghetti
    casserole, 66
    sauce, 19
Stews, see Soups and Stews
Stifado (beef with onions), 43
Stroganoff, economy class, 30
Stuffed cabbage leaves, 19
Stuffing, herbed, 59
Substitutes for
    baking powder, 25
    beef broth, 25
    bread crumbs, dry, 25
    butter, 25
    cereal (chocolate farina), 25
    cheese, natural, 25
    chicken
        broth, 25
        cooked, 25
    chili sauce, 26
    chocolate
        pieces, semisweet for melting
            only, 26
        unsweetened, 26
    cornstarch, 26
    cream
        sour, 26
        whipped, 26
        whipping, 26
    flour
        cake, 26
        for thickening, 26
    garlic, 26
    half-and-half, 26
    herbs, fresh, 26
    honey, 26
    marshmallows, 26
    milk
        sour, 26
        whole, 26
    mustard, prepared, 26
    oil, for frying, 26
    onion, 26
    sugar
        brown, 26
        confectioners', 26

tomato
    juice, 26
    ketchup, 26
    sauce, 26
    tomatoes, 26
    yeast, compressed, 26
Sugar, substitutes for
    brown, 26
    confectioners', 26
Sweetbreads aux capres, 53
Syrup
    artificial maple, 14
    cheaper to do-it-yourself, 14

Tagliarini, 64
Test your food buying I.Q. 5
    answers to, 6
Tongue, meat-cottage cheese mold, 38
Treats, 76
Tuna
    casserole, 55
        and noodle, Florentine, 56
        broccoli and macaroni, 56
        choose-a-partner, 56
        green beans and rice, 56
    -chili chowder, 55
    pie
        blushing, 57
        Swiss and, 70
    supreme, skillet, 55
Turkey
    ABC of leftovers, 36
    creamy seasoned, 39
    fondue sandwiches, 38
    freezer storage limits, 91
    hearty poultry pie, 38

meat-cottage cheese mold, 38
mushroom bake, 40
refrigerator storage limits
    cooked, leftover, 90
    thawed, whole, 90
roasting pan gravy, 59
roast, with cooked giblets, 58
scalloped, 39
soufflé, 38
soup, 39
timetable for roasting, at 325°F, 58
-tomato mac, 65
versatile meat-vegetable casserole, 48

Veal
    bone shapes indicate cooking methods, 47
    refrigerator storage limits
        cooked, 89
        fresh, 90
Vegetables
    ABC of leftovers, 36
    beans
        buckaroo, 73
        Lancaster County lima, 73
    broccoli with horseradish cream, 75
    cabbage
        company, 73
        leaves, stuffed, 19
        slaw, tart, 74
    canned, 72
    carrots Lyonnaise, 75
    casserole
        green bean-pork chop, 51

ground beef-eggplant, 48
pork, macaroni, 40
sweet potato-rice, 66
cheaper to buy in the convenience forms
    commercially canned and frozen, 14
    dried, 14
    freeze-dried, 14
    frozen, 14
    instant mashed potatoes, 14
cheaper to do-it-yourself, 14
freezer storage limits, 91
fresh produce, 72
frozen, 72
hi-style spinach, 74
onion(s)
    glazed, 75
    pie, cheese-, 71
    substitutes for, 26
peppers
    strips, fried green, 75
    stuffed, 74
potato(es)
    O'Brien, 75
    salad, Italian, 74
    refrigerator storage limits
        cooked and canned (opened), 90
        fresh, 90
    tomatoes, substitute for, 26

Waffles, 17
Welsh rabbit in chafing dish, 71

Yeast, compressed, substitute for, 26